THE
EARTH
IN THREE DIMENSIONS

WORLD
ATLAS

BY KEITH LYE
MAPS BY MALCOLM PORTER

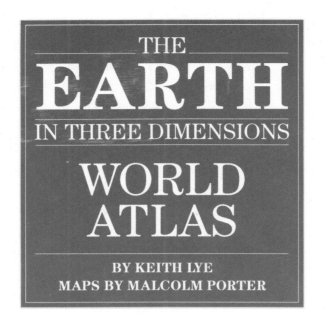

D

DEALERFIELD

CONTENTS

INTRODUCTION 2

OUR CHANGING WORLD 4

THE NORTH POLE AND THE ARCTIC 6

THE SOUTH POLE AND ANTARCTICA 7

NORTH AMERICA 8

CANADA 10

ALASKA 11

THE UNITED STATES AND HAWAII 12

MEXICO, CENTRAL AND SOUTH AMERICA,
AND THE CARIBBEAN 14

EUROPE 16

THE CHANGING FACE OF EUROPE 20

NORTHERN EURASIA 22

SOUTHERN ASIA 24

AFRICA 28

AUSTRALIA AND THE PACIFIC 30

THE HUMAN WORLD 32

CLIMATE 34

THE ENVIRONMENT: POLLUTION OF LAND, SEA
AND ATMOSPHERE 36

WORLD INFORMATION TABLE 38

THE SOLAR SYSTEM 40

INTERNATIONAL TIME ZONES 40

INDEX 41

Dealerfield Limited.
Glaisdale Parkway, Glaisdale Drive,
Nottingham, NG8 4GA

Copyright © 1994 Electric Paper

Publisher: Edward Pitcher
Editor: Veronica Ross
Paper Engineer: David Hawcock
Cartographer and
    Diagram Illustrator: Malcolm Porter
Picture Research: Moira McIlroy
Illustrator (endpapers):   David Hardy

All rights reserved.
A catalogue record for this book is available
from the British Library

Printed in Colombia by Carvajal S.A.
(First Edition) ISBN 1-85927-044-1

Picture acknowledgements

Airbus Industries: 20(bl). **B&C Alexander:** 11.
J.Allan Cash: 20(bc), 34(r). **Duncan Brown:** 10/11.
Colorific: 24(r). **Eurotunnel Press Office:** 20(t). **Eye
Ubiquitous:** 24(l). **Greenpeace:** 37(c). **Image Bank:**
32(r) P.Thomann. **Magnum:** 23, 37(b). **Oxford
Scientific Films:** 15(br). **Science Photo Library:**
6 5(t), 15(t), 37(t). **Spectrum Colour Library:** 8(b),
13,16(b),19(b), 25(l), 26(l), 29(t), 29(br). **Frank
Spooner Pictures:** 20(br), 15(bl) . **Tony Stone
Associates:** 6, 6/7, 7, 8(t), 9,10, 12(b), 12(t, 14(l),
14(r), 16(t), 16(c), 18(t), 18(c), 18(bl), 18(br),19(t),
21(t), 21(b), 22(t), 25(r), 26(r), 27(tl), 27(tr), 27(c),
27(b), 29(bl), 31(bl), 31(br), 32(l), 33(tl), 33(tr), 34(l),
36. **Zefa:** 5(b), 17, 22(b).

INTRODUCTION

THE EARTH IN THREE DIMENSIONS contains a pop-up globe, which shows the Earth as it would look to an astronaut in a distant spacecraft. The globe shows the seven continents, listed in order of size on the facing page, and the oceans which cover over seven-tenths of the Earth's surface.

Like the Earth, the pop-up globe rotates (turns) on its axis (an imaginary line joining the North Pole, the centre of the Earth, and the South Pole). It also shows the equator, an imaginary line running around the globe, exactly half-way between the two poles.

The Atlas

In addition to the three-dimensional globe the atlas has maps of the continents and information about countries, their boundaries, capitals and other large cities, together with natural features, such as rivers, lakes and mountains. The atlas also shows how maps change because of wars and politics. Towards the end of the atlas, we find out how people are polluting our planet.

How to use this Atlas

To find out what the symbols and colours used on the maps mean, look at the key on the facing page. On each page showing the map of a continent, there is also a locater globe with the continent shown in yellow. This will help you find the continent. The scale bar will help you to work out the distance between two places on the map. At the end of the book a table lists country populations, areas and capitals. Square kilometres and miles are sometimes shortened to 'sq km' and 'sq mi'.

Key to the maps

▮	Forests
▮	Farmland/pastures
▮	Deserts
▮	Tundra
▮	Icepack

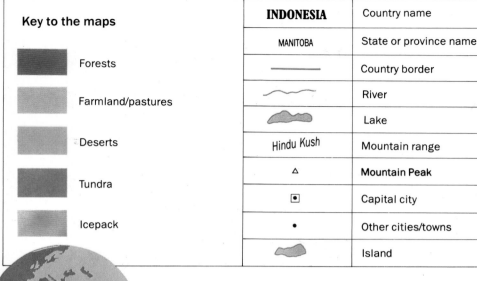

INDONESIA	Country name
MANITOBA	State or province name
——	Country border
〜	River
◯	Lake
Hindu Kush	Mountain range
△	**Mountain Peak**
⊡	Capital city
•	Other cities/towns
◯	Island

miles
0   500
0   500
kilometres

△ *A scale bar.*
◁ *A continent locater globe.*

△ *You will find these colours and symbols on each map, and this table tells you what they mean.*

Maps and Globes

Globes give a true and accurate picture of our Earth. But globes are small. They cannot give us as much information as maps. Maps can also be used to give special information, such as the extent of pollution around the world, as shown on the world maps on pages 36-37. But map-makers face a problem. There is no way of showing the curved surface of the Earth on a flat piece of paper without distorting it in some way. For example, the oval world map shown above could not be stuck on to the surface of a globe.

Map Projections

Map-makers have worked out ways of showing the world, or parts of it, as accurately as possible on flat surfaces. They are called map projections. By using map projections, which are worked out mathematically, map-makers can show some features, such as areas, shapes and distances accurately. But some parts of the world have to be distorted in order to show a world map in one piece.

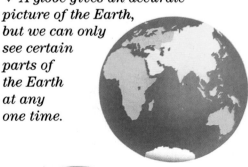

△ *This map projection shows all the continents in the world, but the shapes are not accurate.*
▽ *A globe gives an accurate picture of the Earth, but we can only see certain parts of the Earth at any one time.*

The Continents in brief

Asia: area 44,045,000 sq km (17,006,000 sq mi) population, 3,307,000,000.

Africa: area 30,261,000 sq km (11,684,000 sq mi) population, 664,000,000.

North America: area 24,237,000 sq km (9,358,000 sq mi) population, 433,000,000.

South America: area 17,806,000 sq km (6,875,000 sq mi) population, 304,000,000.

Antarctica: area 14,000,000 sq km (5,400,000 sq mi) population, none permanent.

Europe: area 10,521,000 sq km (4,062,000 sq mi) population, 700,000,000.

Australia: area 7,713,000 sq km (2,978,000 sq mi) population, 17,500,000.

Latitude and Longitude

Every place on Earth can be located by its latitude and longitude. Lines of latitude run east to west round the world. They are measured in degrees north or south of the equator. The equator is an imaginary line halfway between the North and South poles. Lines of longitude run north to south round the world passing through the poles. They are measured in degrees east or west of an imaginary line called the Prime Meridian 0° which runs through London, England.

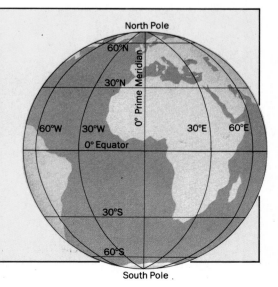

OUR CHANGING WORLD

OUR PLANET EARTH is always changing. Scientists believe that, 500 million years ago, the Earth had land areas and oceans very different from those of today. Over millions of years, the ancient continents moved together. Around 200 million years ago, they came together to form a single landmass, called Pangaea.

Laurasia and Gondwanaland

Around 135 million years ago, Pangaea began to break apart. One block, made up of what is now North America, Europe and most of Asia, split away from Pangaea. Scientists call this northern continent Laurasia. The remaining landmass, consisting of what is now South America, Africa, India, Australia and Antarctica, is called Gondwanaland.

Over the last 135 million years, Laurasia and Gondwanaland have themselves broken apart to form the seven continents in their present positions.

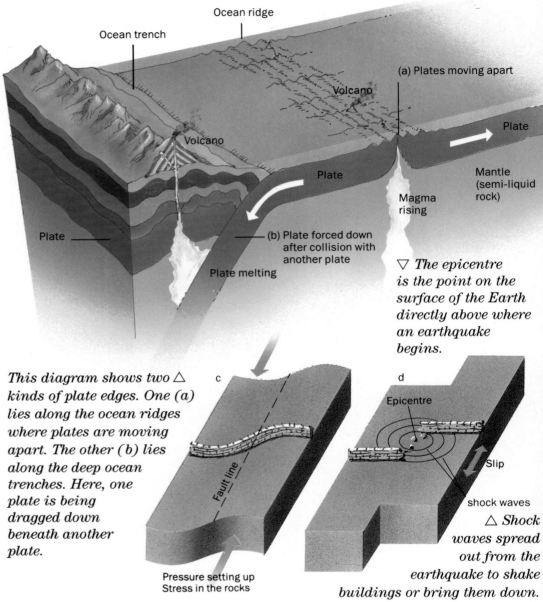

This diagram shows two kinds of plate edges. One (a) lies along the ocean ridges where plates are moving apart. The other (b) lies along the deep ocean trenches. Here, one plate is being dragged down beneath another plate.

▽ *The epicentre is the point on the surface of the Earth directly above where an earthquake begins.*

△ *Shock waves spread out from the earthquake to shake buildings or bring them down.*

△ *Some plates move alongside each other in opposite directions (c). This is called a transform fault. Earthquakes occur when the plates move with a sudden jerk (d).*

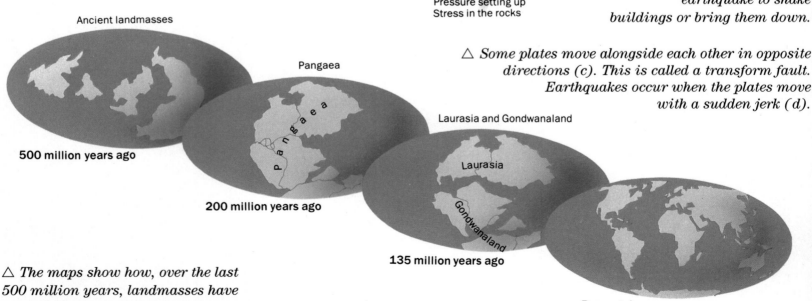

Ancient landmasses
500 million years ago

Pangaea
200 million years ago

Laurasia and Gondwanaland
135 million years ago

Present day

△ *The maps show how, over the last 500 million years, landmasses have moved together and then split up again.*

4

Moving Plates

The Earth's outer layer is split, like a cracked eggshell, into large blocks, or 'plates'. Plates are made up of the hard crust, or outer layer of the Earth, which forms the seabed and the continents.

Under the plates, between 70 and 100 kilometres (43-62 miles) below the surface, is a thick layer of semi-liquid rock called the mantle. Great heat inside the Earth makes this rock move around and this causes the plates to shift position. These movements often result in many mantle to form deep ocean trenches. The descending plate melts into the mantle, but some of the melted rock rises upwards to the surface to form volcanoes. Most of the world's volcanoes are formed in this way. When a volcano erupts, magma, which is called lava on the surface, pours out of the top of the volcano.

Earthquakes

Plates do not move smoothly. For most of the time, their jagged edges are locked together. But when pressure builds up, the plates move, causing earthquakes.

Earthquakes are common around ocean ridges and trenches. They also occur along cracks in the Earth's surface called transform faults. These cracks occur where two plates are moving past each other in opposite directions. The San Andreas Fault, in California, is an example of this kind of transform fault. Movements along the fault cause earthquakes in Los Angeles and San Francisco.

Mountains

Mountains are formed when plates collide. 'Fold mountains' occur when two plates push against each other, squeezing the rocks between them into huge folds. The world's highest range, the Himalayas, was formed when a plate carrying India pushed against the Eurasian plate. Plate movements also fracture (crack) rocks. Blocks of rock pushed up along the faults form 'block mountains'.

▽ A volcano in Russia's Kamchatka peninsula is one of many that circle the Pacific Ocean. These volcanoes form the huge Pacific 'ring of fire'.

earthquakes, volcanoes and the formation of mountain ranges.

Ocean Ridges

Currents in the mantle pull plates slowly apart. When this happens on the ocean floor, hot magma (molten rock) rises up to fill the gaps between the plates. The magma hardens to form long, underwater mountain ridges.

Ocean Trenches

When two plates collide, the edge of one plate is pushed beneath the other and plunged into the hot

△ Movement along the plate edges of the San Andreas Fault have caused major earthquakes, most recently in Los Angeles in 1994. In 1906 the plate edges moved up to 5.5 metres (18 feet) in opposite directions causing an earthquake that destroyed San Francisco.

THE NORTH POLE AND THE ARCTIC

THE ARCTIC includes the Arctic Ocean, the world's smallest ocean, and the northern-most parts of Asia, Europe and North America, which lie north of the Arctic Circle.

The North Pole lies near the centre of the Arctic Ocean. The Arctic has long, bitterly cold winters. Sea ice, which is often called pack ice, covers much of the ocean throughout the year.

△ Polar bears live in the icy Arctic region, hunting seals and other animals for food.

Bering Strait

Arctic Circle

Tundra

Wrangel I.

NORTH AMERICA

Beaufort Sea
Permanent pack ice

New Siberian Is.

Laptev Sea

ASIA

ARCTIC OCEAN

Severnaya Zemlya

North Pole

Ellesmere I.

Kara Sea

Baffin I. Baffin Bay

Novaya Zemlya

Svalbard (Spitsbergen)

GREENLAND

Barents Sea

Norwegian Sea

Iceland

EUROPE

miles
0   500

0   500
kilometres

The Arctic Ocean in brief

Area: about 9,500,000 sq km (about 3,668,000 sq mi).
Greatest known depth: about 5,500 metres (18,045 feet).
Permanent ice cover: about 6,000,000 sq km (2,316,600 sq mi).
Thickness of sea ice: 3-3.5 metres (10-12 feet).

Greenland, the world's largest island, lies in the Arctic. Most of Greenland is covered by a huge ice sheet. Ice and snow cover many Arctic islands throughout the year. The Arctic also includes a treeless region called the tundra, where the snow melts in summer. Plants, such as lichens, mosses, low shrubs and nearly 1,000 kinds of flowers, grow in the tundra region. Animals such as caribou, reindeer and moose graze in the tundra during the summer. Inuit (or Eskimos) live in the Arctic regions of North America.

◁ Scientists work in the cold waters of the Arctic Ocean, recording weather conditions, water temperatures, movements of ice, and evidence of pollution.

THE SOUTH POLE AND ANTARCTICA

ANTARCTICA, the world's fifth largest continent, is bigger than either Europe or Australia. Antarctica surrounds the South Pole and is the coldest continent. The lowest known air temperature, -89.2°C (-128.6°F), was recorded there in 1983.

Most of Antarctica is covered by ice, which is up to 4,800 metres (15,750 feet) thick in places. In some areas, the ice extends over the sea, forming ice shelves. When chunks of the ice break away, they form huge icebergs. One iceberg was larger than the country of Belgium.

The Antarctic Peninsula, which points towards South America, has some ice-free areas where the

△ *Sea ice surrounds much of Antarctica for most of the year.*

continent's only flowering plants are found. No one lives in Antarctica all the time. But scientists from several nations spend periods there in research stations. They study Antarctica's resources and its wildlife, including the many living creatures, such as fish, seals and whales, found in the waters around the continent.

The scientists also record changes in weather conditions, especially those that may affect other parts of the world.

No one owns the land in Antarctica, though several nations claim some areas. The continent has not been developed. Many people would like it to remain a wilderness, or a 'world park', where its animals, including its many penguins, can live in safety.

Antarctica in brief

Highest point: Vinson Massif, 5,140 metres (16,864 feet) above sea level.
Greatest depth of ice: about 4,800 metres (15,750 feet).

miles
0   500

0   500
kilometres

NORTH AMERICA

NORTH AMERICA is the third largest continent after Asia and Africa. It covers about a sixth of the world's land area.

The northern part of North America includes two vast countries, Canada and the United States. In the far northeast lies Greenland, the largest island in the world.

North America also includes Mexico, the seven countries of Central America, which form a land bridge between Mexico and Colombia in South America, and the many tropical islands in the Caribbean Sea. North America is bounded by three oceans, the icy Arctic Ocean in the north, the Pacific Ocean in the west, and the Atlantic Ocean in the east.

North America in brief

Highest point: Mount McKinley, Alaska, 6,194 metres (20,320 feet).
Longest river: Mississippi, 3,766 kilometres (2,340 miles).
Largest lake: Lake Superior, 82,103 square kilometres (31,700 square miles).

North America
(2 countries)
Canada
United States of America (U.S.A.)

◁ *Inuit people live in northern Canada. They catch fish through holes in the ice that covers the sea.*

Brooks Range
Beau[...]
Se[...]
ALASKA (U.S.A.)
DENALI NATIONAL PARK
Yukon
Bering Sea
Alaska
Mt McKinley
Range
Aleutian Islands
Gulf of Alaska
Mt Logan
ROCKY
Mt Robs[...]
GRO[...] MOU[...]
PACIFIC OCEAN
Vancouver
Portland
Mt R[...]
Coastal Ranges
Cascade Range
Sacramento
San Francisco
Mt [...]
Sierra Nevada
San Andreas Fault
Los Angeles
San Dieg[...]

Protecting the Wilderness

Arches National Park in southeastern Utah contains beautiful natural rock formations, such as the Delicate Arch, left. Much of the finest scenery in the United States is now protected in the country's 50 national parks or in smaller areas, such as national monuments. Yellowstone National Park, set up in 1870, was the world's first national park.

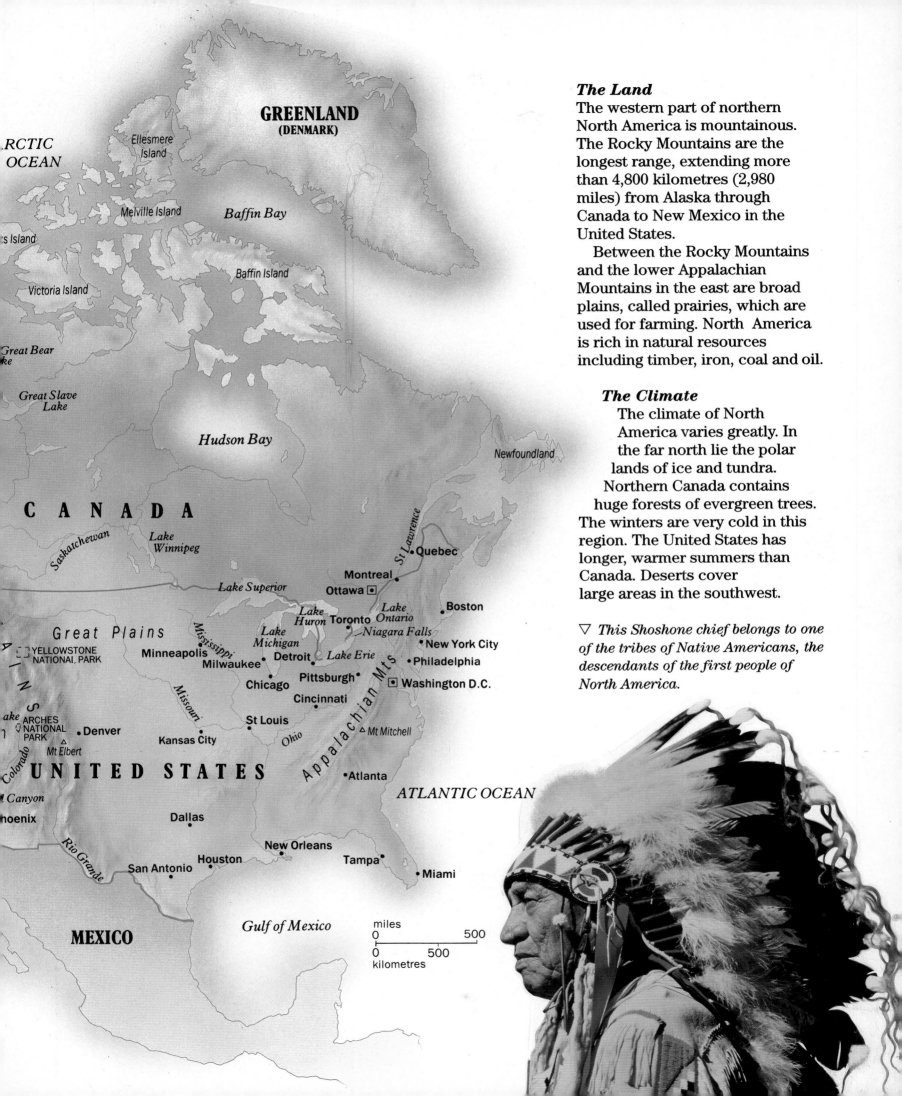

The Land

The western part of northern North America is mountainous. The Rocky Mountains are the longest range, extending more than 4,800 kilometres (2,980 miles) from Alaska through Canada to New Mexico in the United States.

Between the Rocky Mountains and the lower Appalachian Mountains in the east are broad plains, called prairies, which are used for farming. North America is rich in natural resources including timber, iron, coal and oil.

The Climate

The climate of North America varies greatly. In the far north lie the polar lands of ice and tundra. Northern Canada contains huge forests of evergreen trees. The winters are very cold in this region. The United States has longer, warmer summers than Canada. Deserts cover large areas in the southwest.

▽ *This Shoshone chief belongs to one of the tribes of Native Americans, the descendants of the first people of North America.*

GREENLAND
(DENMARK)

ARCTIC
OCEAN

Ellesmere
Island

Melville Island

Baffin Bay

s Island

Baffin Island

Victoria Island

Great Bear
ke

Great Slave
Lake

Hudson Bay

Newfoundland

C A N A D A

Saskatchewan

Lake
Winnipeg

St Lawrence

Quebec

Montreal
Ottawa ⊡

Lake Superior

Boston

Lake
Huron Toronto

Lake
Ontario

Niagara Falls

Lake
Michigan

New York City

Great Plains

Mississippi

Philadelphia

YELLOWSTONE
NATIONAL PARK

Minneapolis
Milwaukee

Detroit

Lake Erie

Pittsburgh

Washington D.C. ⊡

Chicago

Cincinnati

Missouri

Appalachian Mts

ake
ARCHES
NATIONAL
PARK

Denver

St Louis

Ohio

△ Mt Mitchell

Kansas City

Mt Elbert △

Colorado

U N I T E D   S T A T E S

Atlanta

Canyon

ATLANTIC OCEAN

hoenix

Dallas

Rio Grande

New Orleans

Tampa

Houston

Miami

San Antonio

MEXICO

Gulf of Mexico

miles
0   500

0   500
kilometres

CANADA

CANADA is the world's second largest country after the Russian Federation (Russia). It stretches right across North America, from the North Atlantic to the North Pacific Ocean.

Although Canada is a vast country, about 80 per cent of the people live within 300 kilometres (186 miles) of the U.S. border. Far northern Canada is too cold for human settlement.

Canada is divided into ten provinces and two territories, each of which has its own government. The national Parliament meets in the capital, Ottawa. Canada was once part of the British Empire. The people still have strong ties with the United Kingdom and they recognize Queen Elizabeth II as their head of state. The country became self-governing in 1867.

Canada also has strong ties with the United States. In 1994, Canada, the United States and Mexico signed the North American Free Trade Agreement, which has created a huge trading union.

The People
The first people to settle in North America were the ancestors of the Native Americans (also called American Indians). They entered North America from Asia perhaps 40,000 years ago, when the sea level was lower than it is today and the continents were joined by a land bridge.

The Native Americans spread southwards throughout North and South America. Later arrivals, the ancestors of the Inuit people, also came from Asia, but they stayed in the north in what is now Canada

Canadian provinces and capitals

YUKON TERRITORY
Whitehorse
NORTHWEST TERRITORIES
Yellowknife
BRITISH COLUMBIA
ALBERTA
Edmonton
Victoria
SASKATCHEWAN
Regina
MANITOBA
Winnipeg
ONTARIO
NEWFOUNDLAND
St John's
QUEBEC
PRINCE EDWARD ISLAND
Charlottetown
Quebec
Fredericton
NEW BRUNSWICK
NOVA SCOTIA
Halifax
Great Lakes
Ottawa
Toronto

◁ *Quebec is Canada's oldest city and capital of French-speaking Quebec province.*

and Alaska. Today, the Native Americans, including the Inuit, make up only about two per cent of Canada's population. The majority of the people are of European descent. About 37 per cent of Canadians are of British descent. They speak English, one of Canada's two official languages.

The other official language is French, because about 32 per cent of Canadians are of French descent. The province with the largest French-speaking population is Quebec, where many people have said that they want to establish their own independent country.

Other large groups of people are of German, Italian and Ukrainian descent. In recent years, many Asian immigrants have settled in Canada.

◁ *Grouse Mountain is a ski resort on Vancouver's north shore. Vancouver, one of Canada's largest cities, is a major port in the province of British Columbia.*

The Economy
Canada has plenty of fertile farmland, vast forests, and rich reserves of many minerals. It is a wealthy country and its people enjoy high standards of living. About 77 per cent of Canadians live in cities and towns. The largest cities, Toronto and Montreal, are in the country's main industrial region which lies near the Great Lakes and in the St. Lawrence River valley.

ALASKA

ALASKA is the largest state in the United States. But it comes 49th among the states in population. Only Wyoming has fewer people.

Nearly a third of Alaska lies in the Arctic region. Winters are long and cold, but some crops can grow during the short summers. Large areas of wilderness have been set aside as national parks. The Denali National Park includes Mount McKinley, the highest mountain in North America.

Southern Alaska and the Aleutian Islands contain active volcanoes. The area is also hit from time to time by severe earthquakes.

The People
Alaska has a population of about 550,000 people. This figure includes about 74,000 Native Americans – about 50,000 Inuit and 24,000 American Indians. Most of the other people who live in Alaska are of European descent.

The 49th State
The western tip of mainland Alaska is only 82 kilometres (51 miles) from Russia, which once owned Alaska. But, in 1867, the United States bought the territory for US $7.2 million.

Many Americans thought that this was a waste of money. The purchase of Alaska was called Seward's Folly, after William H. Seward, the American Secretary of State who was responsible for buying the area. But Alaska's rich resources, including oil, minerals and timber, have repaid the purchase price many times over.

Alaska finally became a state of the United States on January 3, 1959. It became the 49th state, seven months before Hawaii achieved statehood as the 50th state on August 21, 1959.

▽ *Sleds drawn by husky dogs are sometimes still used for transport in Alaska and northern Canada.*

THE UNITED STATES AND HAWAII

THE UNITED STATES is the world's fourth largest country, after Russia, Canada and China. It is divided into 50 states, each of which has its own government. The national government is based in the country's capital, Washington D.C. The letters D.C. stand for the District of Columbia, a special area which was set aside for the capital city.

During the 16th and 17th centuries, many Europeans migrated to North America and settled. The British gradually gained control over much of North America. The United States was created when American colonists fought the War of Independence against British control. The war officially ended in 1783.

The new nation grew rapidly during the 19th century. Today it ranks third after China and India in population. The United States is world renowned for its many achievements in the fields of science, technology and entertainment; for example, the space programme based at Cape Canaveral in Florida and the Hollywood film industry.

Hawaii

Hawaii became the 50th state of America in 1959. It is the only state which is not on the North American mainland.

Hawaii consists of eight large and 124 small islands, which lie in the North Pacific Ocean. All the islands are formed by volcanoes that rise from the sea floor.

The only active volcanoes today are on the largest island, which is also called Hawaii. Hawaii is a beautiful state, which attracts many tourists. The original people of Hawaii are Polynesians, but today people of Polynesian descent make up only about 15 per cent of the population. People descended from Europeans, Japanese, and other Asians make up the rest. The capital of the state is Honolulu, on Oahu Island.

▽ *Buffalo once roamed on the prairies where wheat is now grown on highly efficient farms.*

△ *California's redwoods are the tallest trees in the world. The largest tree on earth is a redwood named 'Howard A. Libby'.*

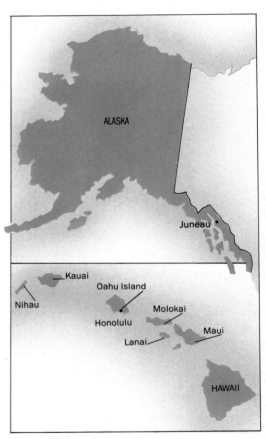

ALASKA

Juneau

Kauai

Nihau

Oahu Island

Honolulu

Molokai

Lanai

Maui

HAWAII

The People

Native Americans, the first people in North America, now make up less than one per cent of the population of the United States, while people of European origin, who began to settle in the 16th century, make up about 80 per cent.

12

African Americans, the descendants of slaves, are the largest minority group in the United States, making up about 12 per cent of the population. Other groups include people whose ancestors came from Asia and various Pacific islands.

The Economy

The United States is a rich country. It produces more agricultural produce, including maize, wheat and soya beans, than any other country in the world.

But most people live in cities, where they work in manufacturing and service industries. Pittsburgh, in the northeast, is one of the largest industrial cities with iron, steel and chemical plants. The computer industry is concentrated in California on the West Coast, while Detroit is known as the 'automobile capital' of the world, producing 25 per cent of the world's cars and trucks.

The country's largest cities include New York City, Los Angeles, Chicago, Houston and Philadelphia.

▷ *The New York City skyline by night is one of the world's most glittering sights.*

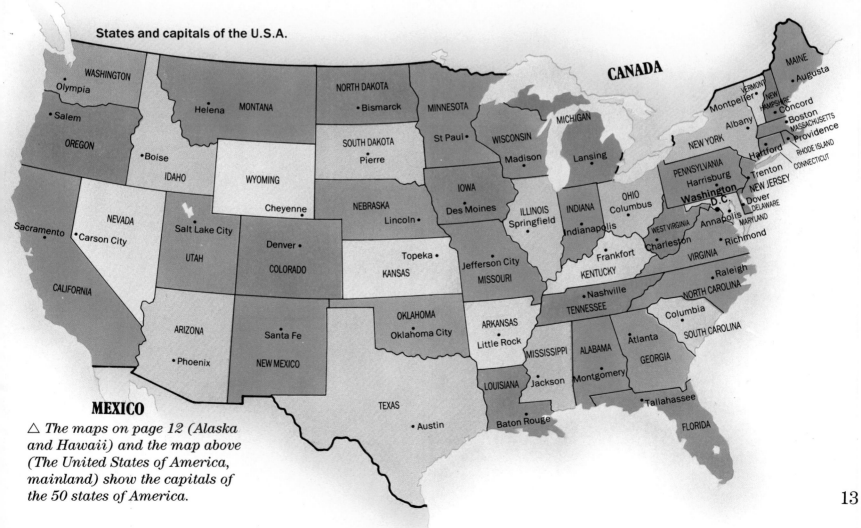

States and capitals of the U.S.A.

△ *The maps on page 12 (Alaska and Hawaii) and the map above (The United States of America, mainland) show the capitals of the 50 states of America.*

MEXICO, CENTRAL AND SOUTH AMERICA, AND THE CARIBBEAN

THE HUGE REGION extending from Mexico to the tip of South America, is called Latin America. This is because most people speak Spanish, French or Portuguese languages which developed from Latin, the language of Ancient Rome. A few non-Latin European languages and many Native American languages are spoken in some areas.

Mexico and Central America

The land in Mexico and Central America is mainly mountainous, with high volcanoes.

Northern Mexico contains deserts, but the climate of most of the region is warm and rainy. Modern Mexico City is one of the largest cities in the world.

The Caribbean

The islands of the Caribbean, which are also called the West Indies, have a warm climate. Farming is a major activity, but tourism is also important. Tourists are attracted by the beaches, magnificent scenery and the fine weather.

Mexico, Central and South America, and the Caribbean
(33 countries)

Antigua & Barbuda	Haiti
Argentina	Honduras
Bahamas	Jamaica
Barbados	Mexico
Belize	Nicaragua
Bolivia	Panama
Brazil	Paraguay
Chile	Peru
Colombia	St. Kitts
Costa Rica	– Nevis
Cuba	St. Lucia
Dominica	St. Vincent
Dominican	& the
Republic	Grenadines
Ecuador	Surinam
El Salvador	Trinidad
Grenada	& Tobago
Guatemala	Uruguay
Guyana	Venezuela

South America

South America, the fourth largest continent, contains the world's longest mountain chain, the Andes.

The climate varies greatly, hot rainforests in the north, deserts on the coasts of northern Chile and Peru, and grasslands in the south. The far south contains a cold desert region called Patagonia. Sugar cane, tobacco and coffee are grown on large plantations. South America also has natural reserves of gold, silver, copper, tin and lead.

South America in brief

Highest point: Aconcagua, Argentina, 6,959 metres (22,831 feet).
Longest river: Amazon, 6,437 kilometres (4,000 miles).
Largest lake: Lake Maracaibo, Venezuela, 13,512 square kilometres (5,217 square miles).

△ *Before the Panama Canal was completed in 1914, ships sailing between the Atlantic and Pacific Oceans travelled around South America. The canal shortened the journey between New York and San Francisco by 12,600 kilometres (7,830 miles).*

Native American Civilizations

Several Native American civilizations existed in Central and South America long before the arrival of Europeans. The Mayans and Toltecs built pyramids with temples on top of them in Mexico and parts of Central America. Chichén Itzá in Mexico, below, is a fine example of a Mayan city.

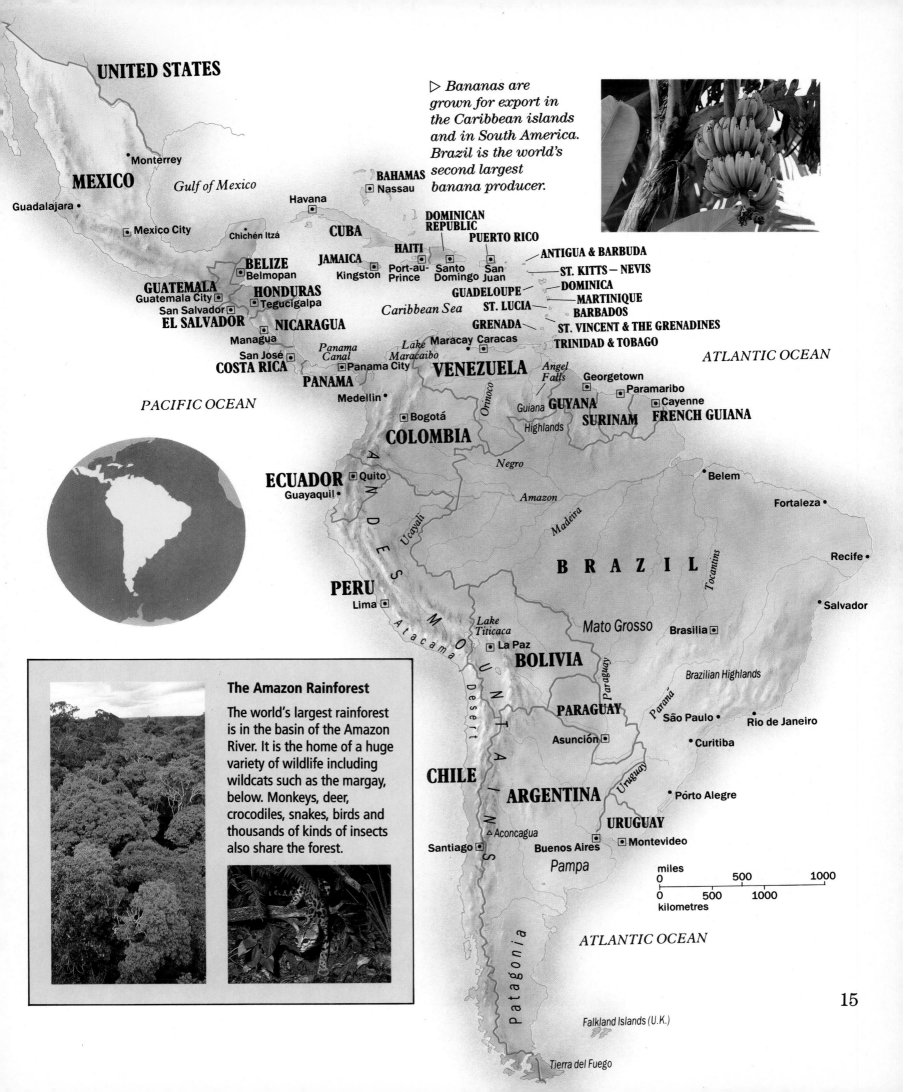

UNITED STATES

· Monterrey

MEXICO   *Gulf of Mexico*

Guadalajara ·

□ Mexico City

Chichén Itzá

BAHAMAS
□ Nassau

Havana
○

CUBA

DOMINICAN
REPUBLIC

PUERTO RICO

HAITI

JAMAICA
□ Belmopan   Kingston   Port-au-   Santo   San
BELIZE   Prince   Domingo   Juan

GUATEMALA
Guatemala City □
San Salvador ·

HONDURAS
□ Tegucigalpa

EL SALVADOR   □ NICARAGUA

Managua ·

▷ Bananas are grown for export in the Caribbean islands and in South America. Brazil is the world's second largest banana producer.

ANTIGUA & BARBUDA
ST. KITTS – NEVIS
DOMINICA
GUADELOUPE
MARTINIQUE
ST. LUCIA   BARBADOS
GRENADA   ST. VINCENT & THE GRENADINES
TRINIDAD & TOBAGO

Caribbean Sea

Panama Canal   Lake Maracaibo   Maracay   Caracas

San José ·

COSTA RICA   □ Panama City

PANAMA

Medellin ·

PACIFIC OCEAN

VENEZUELA   Angel Falls

Orinoco

Guiana   GUYANA
Highlands   SURINAM

Georgetown
□   □ Paramaribo

□ Cayenne

FRENCH GUIANA

ATLANTIC OCEAN

□ Bogotá

COLOMBIA

Negro

ECUADOR   □ Quito

Guayaquil ·

Amazon

· Belem

Madeira

· Fortaleza

A N D E S

Ucayali

PERU

Lima □

Lake
Titicaca

B R A Z I L

Tocantins

· Recife

· Salvador

Atacama

· La Paz

Mato Grosso

Brasilia □

BOLIVIA

Paraguay

Brazilian Highlands

M O U N T A I N S

PARAGUAY

Paraná

São Paulo ·

· Rio de Janeiro

Asunción □

· Curitiba

CHILE

ARGENTINA

Uruguay

· Pôrto Alegre

URUGUAY
□ Montevideo

△ Aconcagua

Santiago □   Buenos Aires ·

Pampa

D e s e r t

P a t a g o n i a

ATLANTIC OCEAN

miles
0   500   1000
0   500   1000
kilometres

The Amazon Rainforest

The world's largest rainforest is in the basin of the Amazon River. It is the home of a huge variety of wildlife including wildcats such as the margay, below. Monkeys, deer, crocodiles, snakes, birds and thousands of kinds of insects also share the forest.

Falkland Islands (U.K.)

Tierra del Fuego

15

EUROPE

EUROPE is the sixth largest continent, but in population it ranks second among the seven continents after Asia.

Europe contains 39 complete independent nations, together with 25 per cent of Russia and 3 per cent of Turkey. Russia is by far the largest country in Europe. Like Ukraine, Europe's second

◁ *Buckingham Palace, home of the British Royal Family, is in London, capital of the United Kingdom. The palace, completed in 1836, has 600 rooms including a ballroom 34 metres (111 feet) long.*

△ *Flowers grown in the Netherlands are sold in countries all over the world.*

Europe in brief

Highest point: Mount Elbrus, in the Caucasus Mountains, Russia, 5,633 metres (18,481 feet).

Longest river: Volga, in Russia, 3,531 kilometres (2,194 miles).

Largest lake: Caspian Sea, which lies partly in Europe and partly in Asia, 372,000 square kilometres (143,630 square miles).

Other European countries which were also parts of the Soviet Union – Belarus, Moldova, Russia and Ukraine are shown on the map of Eurasia on pages 22-23.

European Mini States

Europe contains some extremely small countries. Vatican City, which covers only 0.44 square kilometres (0.17 square miles) in the Italian capital city of Rome, *continued on page 18*

largest country, it was formerly part of the Soviet Union. Other large countries in Europe include France, Spain, Sweden, Norway and Germany.

The Map of Europe

The map on the opposite page shows 39 of Europe's countries, including Estonia, Latvia and Lithuania. These three countries were also part of the Soviet Union between 1940 and 1991.

△ *Completed in 1889, the Eiffel Tower in Paris was the tallest structure in the world until 1931.*

Europe (39 countries)

Albania	Liechtenstein
Andorra	Lithuania
Austria	Luxembourg
Belgium	Macedonia
Bosnia & Hercegovina	Malta
Bulgaria	Monaco
Croatia	Netherlands
Czech Republic	Norway
Denmark	Poland
Estonia	Portugal
Finland	Romania
France	San Marino
Germany	Slovakia
Greece	Slovenia
Hungary	Spain
Iceland	Sweden
Ireland	Switzerland
Italy	United Kingdom
Latvia	Vatican City
	Yugoslavia*

*Yugoslavia now comprises Serbia and Montenegro only

ICELAND
Reykjavik

North Cape

Norwegian Sea

miles
0   500
0
kilometres   500

Faroe Is.

NORWAY   FINLAND

ATLANTIC OCEAN

Oslo   SWEDEN   Helsinki
                Stockholm

                                        Tallinn   RUSSIAN
SCOTLAND   ESTONIA   FEDERATION
Edinburgh
                        North Sea   LATVIA
N. IRELAND   DENMARK   Riga
        Belfast   Copenhagen   *Baltic Sea*
IRELAND UNITED   LITHUANIA
        KINGDOM   Kaliningrad
Dublin   (RUSSIA)   Vilnius   BELARUS

WALES   Hamburg
        ENGLAND   NETHERLANDS   Berlin   Warsaw
Cardiff   Amsterdam   *Elbe*   POLAND
        London
                        Brussels   Bonn
                        BELGIUM   *Rhine* GERMANY

                        LUXEMBOURG   Prague   UKRAINE
                        Paris   CZECH REP.
        Loire   SLOVAKIA
                                                Munich Vienna Bratislava
        FRANCE   LIECHTENSTEIN   Budapest   MOLDOVA
Bay of Biscay   Bern   P   S AUSTRIA
                SWITZERLAND   A   SLOVENIA HUNGARY
                Lyon   *Rhône*   L   Ljubljana Zagreb   ROMANIA
                        Mt Blanc   P   *Po*   Bucharest
                                                S   CROATIA
PORTUGAL   ANDORRA   ITALY   BOSNIA &   Belgrade
        Pyrenees   Marseille MONACO   HERCEGOVINA   *Danube*
        Ebro   SAN MARINO   Sarajevo
Madrid   YUGOSLAVIA BULGARIA
        Barcelona   *Corsica*   Rome   Sofia
Lisbon SPAIN   VATICAN   Skopje
                                        Sardinia CITY   Tiranë MACEDONIA
        Balearic Is.   ALBANIA
Gibraltar   GREECE
(U.K.)   *Mediterranean Sea*   TURKEY

A F R I C A   *Sicily*   Athens
                MALTA

                                Crete

17

◁ The Rhine, which flows through Germany, is one of Europe's most important waterways. Barges carry raw materials to factories and transport goods to the sea. Many ancient castles can be seen on the banks of the river.

▽ Deep valleys called fiords run far inland along Norway's coasts. These valleys were worn away by rivers of ice called glaciers.

The Land and Climate

Southern Europe has much fine scenery and high mountain ranges. The highest range, the Alps, runs from France, through Switzerland, Italy and southern Germany, into Austria.

A broad plain stretches across central Europe, from northern France through north-central Europe to the Ural Mountains in Russia. To the north, Norway and Sweden have mountains, but Finland is low-lying, with many sparkling lakes and thick forests.

The climate varies greatly from the warm lands around the Mediterranean Sea to the icy Arctic region in the north. Europe's western coasts have a mild climate, by contrast with the hot summers and bitterly cold winters in the east.

is the world's smallest independent country. It is the world headquarters of the Roman Catholic Church and it is ruled by the Pope. Monaco, Europe's second smallest country, is a tiny resort area on the southeast coast of France. The third smallest country, San Marino, is the world's oldest republic. It lies in northeastern Italy.

▽ Although Spain is now swiftly modernizing, its old towns and cities reflect its rich and varied past.

▽ Venice, in northeast Italy, is a city built on islands in the Adriatic Sea. The people use boats instead of buses to get around.

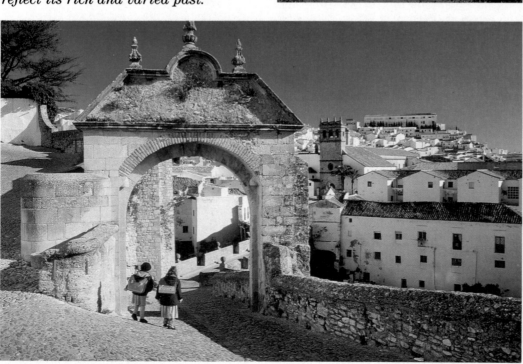

The People

The European part of Russia contains about 120 million people. Germany, with about 80 million people, has Europe's second largest population.

About 50 languages are spoken in Europe. The main language groups are: Romance languages, including French, Italian, Romanian and Spanish; Germanic languages including Danish,

△ Athens in Greece contains the ruins of the Parthenon, a temple built by the Ancient Greeks.

English, German and Swedish; and Balto-Slavic languages, including Bulgarian, Czech, Polish and Russian.

Christianity is Europe's main religion, with Roman Catholics forming the largest group. Members of Orthodox Christian churches live mainly in the southeast and east, including Russia. Europe also has many Protestants, Muslims, Jews and people of other faiths.

Europe has beautiful cities where old buildings stand next to modern ones. Some cities in southern Europe have ruins from great civilizations, such as Ancient Greece and Ancient Rome.

The Economy

Europe's many resources include coal, oil, natural gas and many metals. Some countries, such as Belgium, France, Germany, Italy, the Netherlands, Spain, Sweden and the United Kingdom, have large industries, making such things as aircraft, cars, chemicals, machinery and textiles. Some people still make a living from farming, growing such crops as barley, fruits, potatoes, sugar beet and wheat. Tourism is a major industry.

The map ▷ shows how the former country of Yugoslavia split up into five separate countries in the early 1990s.

△ The map of eastern Europe has changed in recent years. Germany has been reunited, while Czechoslovakia and Yugoslavia have been divided. The former Soviet Union now consists of 15 independent republics.

▽ Prague, capital of the Czech Republic, is one of the most beautiful and historic cities of Europe.

19

THE CHANGING FACE OF EUROPE

THE END OF World War II in 1945 brought about dramatic changes in Europe. The boundaries of several countries were changed and millions of refugees wandered around the continent seeking new homes.

In the late 1940s, the countries of Europe became divided into groups – the East and the West. Communist governments, with strong links with the former Soviet Union, took control of Albania,

Bulgaria, Czechoslovakia, East Germany, Hungary, Poland, Romania and Yugoslavia.

The border between the Western nations and the Communist East was called the 'Iron Curtain' because it was difficult for anyone to pass over to the West from what became known as the 'Eastern Bloc'.

Europe Rebuilds

In 1945, the economies of many European countries were devastated. The United States provided aid, but progress was slow as Europeans worked to rebuild their countries.

In 1952, Belgium, France, Italy, Luxembourg, the Netherlands and West Germany set up the European Coal and Steel Community (ECSC) in an effort to restore their industries.

The European Community

In 1957, the success of the ECSC led the six countries to form the European Economic Community (EEC). The EEC worked to remove barriers which prevented movement of goods and workers between the countries. In this way, they could compete with rich nations, such as the United States. In 1967, the EEC was renamed the European Community.

New Members

Denmark, Ireland and the United Kingdom joined the European Community in 1973, Greece joined in 1981, and Portugal and Spain became members in 1989. In 1990, East Germany was reunited with West Germany and became a member of the Community. In 1993, the European Community was renamed the European Union.

△ *Shuttle trains operate services through the Channel Tunnel. The tunnel links the United Kingdom and France.*

▽ *Increasing co-operation among West European nations led to the building of jumbo jets called airbuses.*

The Berlin Wall

At the end of World War II, Berlin, Germany's capital, was divided by the victorious allies into four zones. These later became two zones; Communist East Berlin and non-Communist West Berlin. The East Germans built a wall between the two zones to stop people fleeing into West Berlin to escape the Communist regime. In 1989, in scenes of great rejoicing, the East German people smashed down the wall, and in 1990 East and West Germany were reunited as a single democratic state.

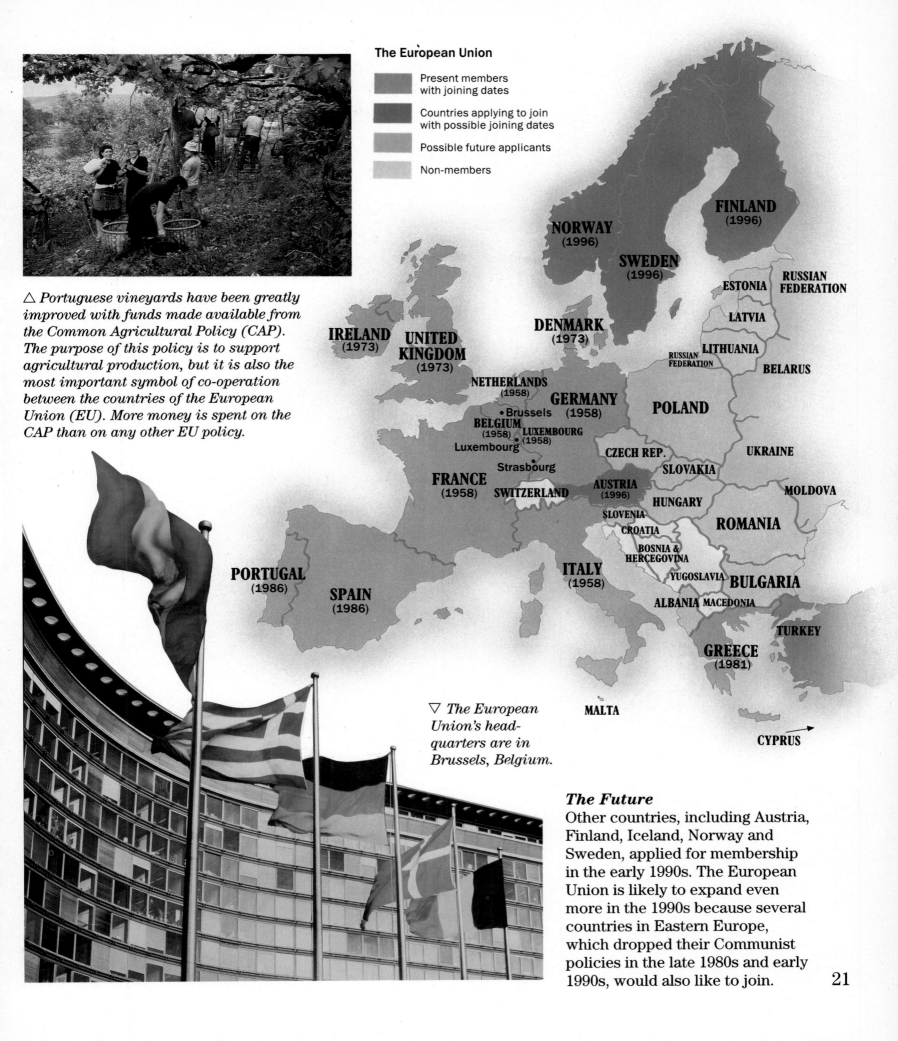

△ *Portuguese vineyards have been greatly improved with funds made available from the Common Agricultural Policy (CAP). The purpose of this policy is to support agricultural production, but it is also the most important symbol of co-operation between the countries of the European Union (EU). More money is spent on the CAP than on any other EU policy.*

The European Union

- Present members with joining dates
- Countries applying to join with possible joining dates
- Possible future applicants
- Non-members

NORWAY (1996)
SWEDEN (1996)
FINLAND (1996)
RUSSIAN FEDERATION
ESTONIA
LATVIA
LITHUANIA
RUSSIAN FEDERATION
BELARUS
DENMARK (1973)
IRELAND (1973)
UNITED KINGDOM (1973)
NETHERLANDS (1958)
GERMANY (1958)
POLAND
• Brussels
BELGIUM (1958)
LUXEMBOURG (1958)
Luxembourg
CZECH REP.
SLOVAKIA
UKRAINE
Strasbourg
FRANCE (1958)
SWITZERLAND
AUSTRIA (1996)
HUNGARY
MOLDOVA
SLOVENIA
CROATIA
ROMANIA
BOSNIA & HERCEGOVINA
PORTUGAL (1986)
SPAIN (1986)
ITALY (1958)
YUGOSLAVIA
BULGARIA
ALBANIA MACEDONIA
TURKEY
GREECE (1981)
MALTA
CYPRUS

▽ *The European Union's head-quarters are in Brussels, Belgium.*

The Future
Other countries, including Austria, Finland, Iceland, Norway and Sweden, applied for membership in the early 1990s. The European Union is likely to expand even more in the 1990s because several countries in Eastern Europe, which dropped their Communist policies in the late 1980s and early 1990s, would also like to join.

21

Northern Eurasia

ASIA, the world's largest continent, is joined to Europe. The border with Europe that follows the Ural Mountains is one of the richest sources of metals in the world; it was a prime source of gold for the Ancient Greeks. The other border following the Caucasus Mountains has been fought over for thousands of years. It is said that 72 languages were once spoken in the region.

The map shows part of Europe in the west, with northern Asia in the east. This huge region is called Northern Eurasia. It includes the Russian Federation, or Russia, the world's largest country. About a quarter of Russia is in Europe and three-quarters is in Asia.

The 12 countries in Northern Eurasia were once part of the Soviet Union. They became separate countries when the Soviet Union broke up in 1991.

△ *St. Basil's Cathedral, facing Red Square in the heart of Moscow, was a museum under Communist rule. Christian services can now be held in the church.*

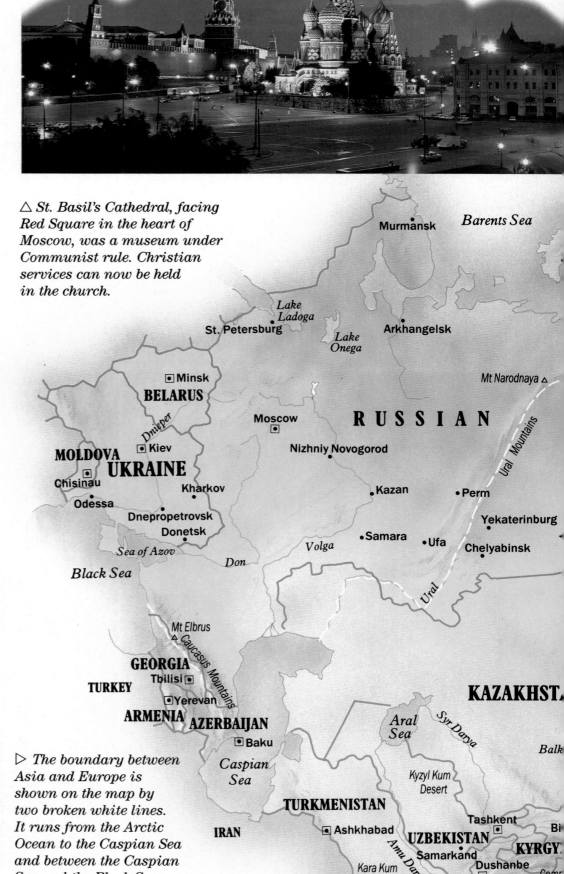

▽ *Samarkand was a centre of Islamic culture for several centuries. Its beautiful mosques are now major tourist attractions.*

▷ *The boundary between Asia and Europe is shown on the map by two broken white lines. It runs from the Arctic Ocean to the Caspian Sea and between the Caspian Sea and the Black Sea.*

22

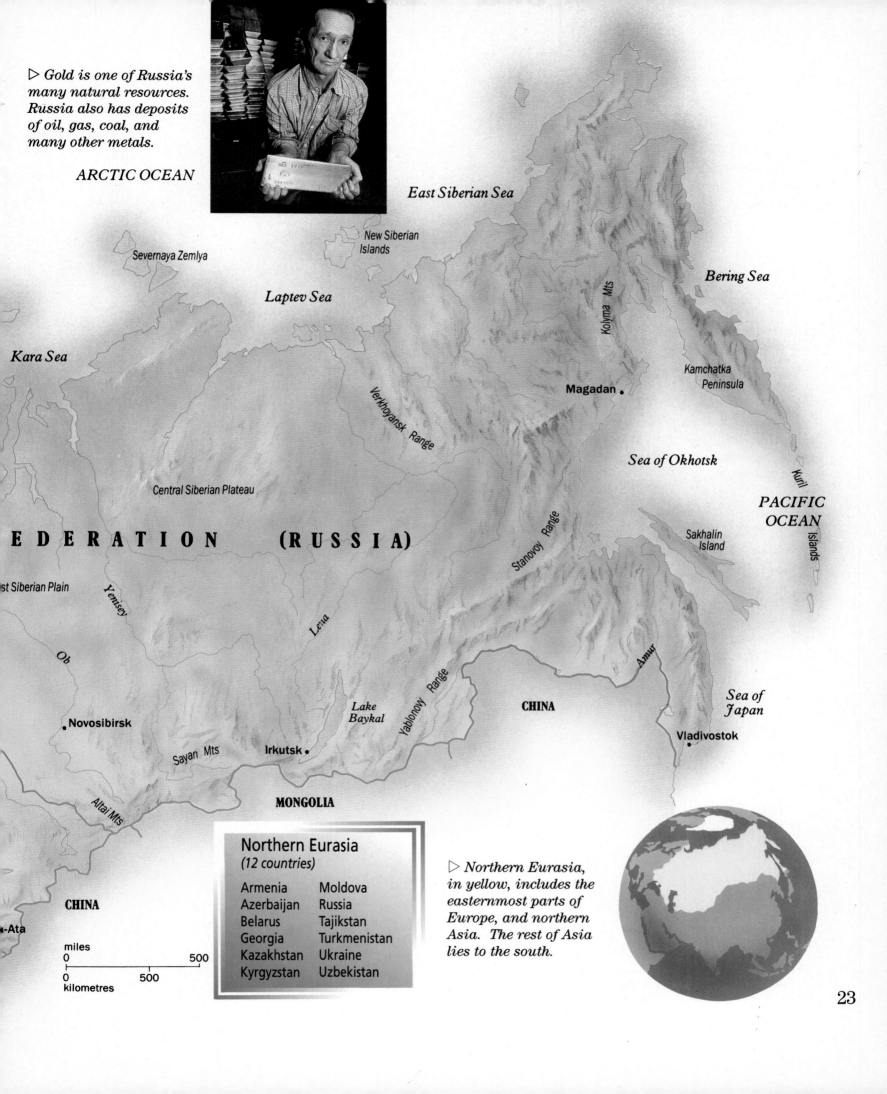

▷ *Gold is one of Russia's many natural resources. Russia also has deposits of oil, gas, coal, and many other metals.*

ARCTIC OCEAN

East Siberian Sea

New Siberian Islands

Severnaya Zemlya

Bering Sea

Laptev Sea

Kolyma Mts

Kara Sea

Kamchatka Peninsula

Verkhoyansk Range

Magadan .

Sea of Okhotsk

Central Siberian Plateau

Kuril Islands

E D E R A T I O N   (R U S S I A)

PACIFIC OCEAN

Stanovoy Range

Sakhalin Island

st Siberian Plain

Yenisey

Lena

Amur

Sea of Japan

Ob

Yablonovy Range

Novosibirsk

Lake Baykal

CHINA

Vladivostok

Sayan Mts

Irkutsk .

MONGOLIA

Altai Mts

CHINA

-Ata

Northern Eurasia
(12 countries)

Armenia	Moldova
Azerbaijan	Russia
Belarus	Tajikstan
Georgia	Turkmenistan
Kazakhstan	Ukraine
Kyrgyzstan	Uzbekistan

▷ *Northern Eurasia, in yellow, includes the easternmost parts of Europe, and northern Asia. The rest of Asia lies to the south.*

miles
0   500

0   500
kilometres

SOUTHERN ASIA

SOUTHERN ASIA has more people than any other continent. It includes China and India, which have more people than any other countries.

The continent contains Russia, China, India and Kazakhstan, four of the world's ten largest countries. But it also has some small countries, including the Maldives, an island nation off the southwest coast of India; Singapore, an island nation in southeastern Asia; and Bahrain, in southwestern Asia.

Asia has many ancient traditions. Farming probably began in southwestern Asia and the earliest civilizations developed in the valleys of the Tigris and Euphrates rivers in what is now Iraq. Other civilizations developed later in the Indus Valley in India and in the Huang He and Chang Jiang Valleys in eastern China.

Religions
Asia was also the birthplace of the world's major religions including Buddhism, Christianity, Judaism, continued on page 26

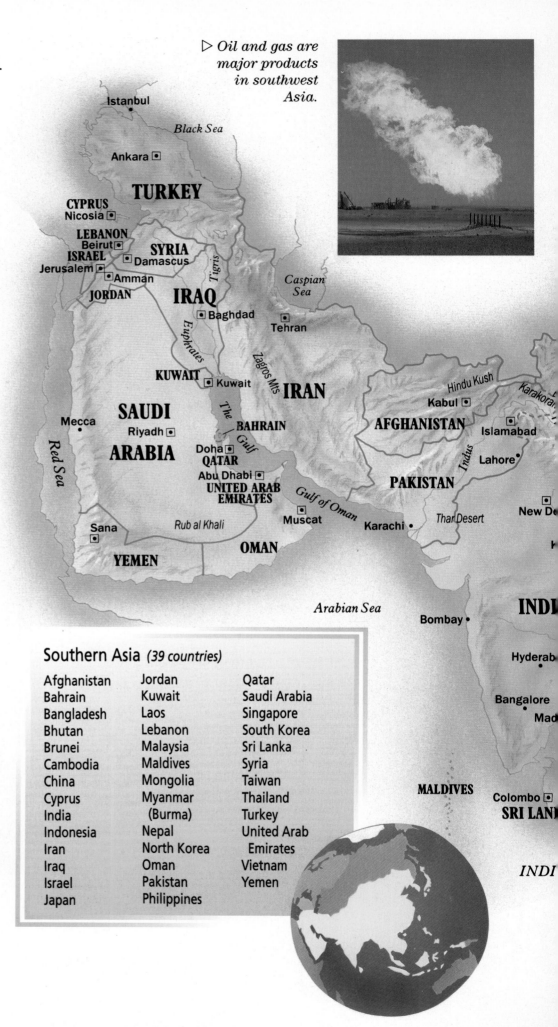

▷ *Oil and gas are major products in southwest Asia.*

△ *Rice is the leading food crop in south-central, southeastern and eastern Asia. Rice grows in warm, wet climates, as here in Sri Lanka.*

Southern Asia (39 countries)

Afghanistan	Jordan	Qatar
Bahrain	Kuwait	Saudi Arabia
Bangladesh	Laos	Singapore
Bhutan	Lebanon	South Korea
Brunei	Malaysia	Sri Lanka
Cambodia	Maldives	Syria
China	Mongolia	Taiwan
Cyprus	Myanmar	Thailand
India	(Burma)	Turkey
Indonesia	Nepal	United Arab
Iran	North Korea	Emirates
Iraq	Oman	Vietnam
Israel	Pakistan	Yemen
Japan	Philippines	

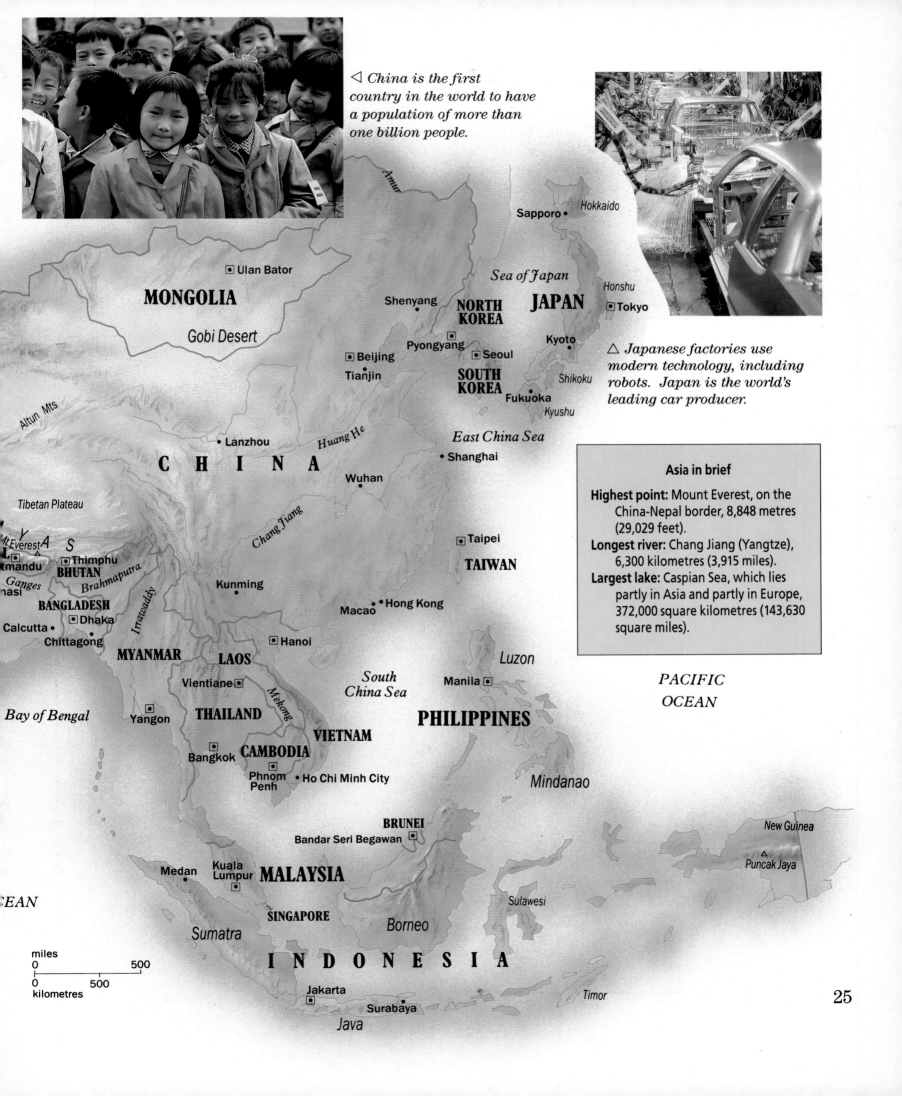

◁ China is the first country in the world to have a population of more than one billion people.

△ Japanese factories use modern technology, including robots. Japan is the world's leading car producer.

MONGOLIA

Gobi Desert

☉ Ulan Bator

Amur

Sapporo • Hokkaido

Sea of Japan

Shenyang •

NORTH KOREA

JAPAN

Honshu

☉ Tokyo

Pyongyang ☉

Kyoto

☉ Beijing

☉ Seoul

Tianjin •

SOUTH KOREA

Shikoku

Fukuoka •

Kyushu

Altun Mts

Lanzhou •

Huang He

East China Sea

C H I N A

• Shanghai

Wuhan •

Tibetan Plateau

Chang Jiang

H I M A L A Y A S

Mt Everest △

☉ Thimphu

Kathmandu ☉

BHUTAN

Ganges

Brahmaputra

nasi

BANGLADESH

Calcutta •

☉ Dhaka

Chittagong •

Irrawaddy

Kunming •

☉ Taipei

TAIWAN

• Hong Kong

Macao •

MYANMAR

LAOS

Vientiane ☉

☉ Hanoi

Mekong

Yangon ☉

THAILAND

South China Sea

Luzon

Manila ☉

Bay of Bengal

Bangkok ☉

CAMBODIA

VIETNAM

Phnom Penh ☉

• Ho Chi Minh City

PHILIPPINES

PACIFIC OCEAN

Mindanao

BRUNEI

Bandar Seri Begawan ☉

New Guinea

△ Puncak Jaya

Medan •

Kuala Lumpur ☉

MALAYSIA

CEAN

SINGAPORE

Borneo

Sulawesi

Sumatra

I N D O N E S I A

miles
0   500

0   500
kilometres

Jakarta ☉

Timor

Surabaya •

Java

Asia in brief

Highest point: Mount Everest, on the China-Nepal border, 8,848 metres (29,029 feet).
Longest river: Chang Jiang (Yangtze), 6,300 kilometres (3,915 miles).
Largest lake: Caspian Sea, which lies partly in Asia and partly in Europe, 372,000 square kilometres (143,630 square miles).

Confucianism, Hinduism and Islam. Shinto is an important religion in Japan.

The Land and Climate

The land of Asia is the most varied in the world. It has many mountain ranges, including the world's highest, the Himalayas. The

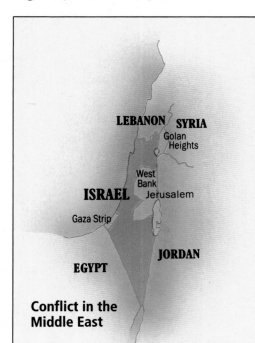

LEBANON SYRIA
Golan Heights

West Bank
ISRAEL Jerusalem

Gaza Strip

JORDAN

EGYPT

Conflict in the Middle East

Arabs and Israeli Jews have fought over the Golan Heights, the Gaza strip and the River Jordan's West Bank since 1948, when modern Israel was created. Holy to Jews, Muslims and Christians, Jerusalem is capital of Israel, and its Dome of the Rock, below, is one of Islam's holiest shrines. In 1994, Israel took the first steps to peace by withdrawing from some of the Arab-claimed lands.

Himalayas contain Mount Everest, which at 8,848 metres (29,029 feet) is the world's highest peak.

Asia also has many lowlands, especially in the north, where evergreen forests cover large areas on the thinly populated plains and low plateaus of Russia. Southern Asia also has large lowlands, where enormous numbers of people live.

The climate also varies greatly. The far north lies in the Arctic region. It has a bitterly cold climate, with long winters. Southern Asia lies near the equator. This region along with south-central and southeastern

▷ *The Taj Mahal, in northern India, is the country's best-known building. It is a tomb built by an Indian ruler, Shah Jehan, in memory of his wife, Mumtaz Mahal. Both of their bodies are buried beneath this beautiful tomb.*

Asia is hot and wet. By contrast, hot deserts cover large areas in southwestern Asia.

Cold deserts, such as the Gobi Desert in Mongolia, occur in the interior. The Tibetan plateau, north of the Himalayas, is one of the bleakest places on Earth.

The People

Asia has a great variety of people, including Muslim Turks and Arabs in the southwest, Hindu Indians in south-central Asia, and Chinese and Japanese in the east. The

continent has a huge number of languages. India alone has 14 major languages, plus around 1,000 minor languages and dialects.

Language, religious, political and other differences have led to conflict between peoples. For example, the Jewish people of Israel have fought wars with Arab nations to preserve their country. In southern Asia, conflict between Hindus and Muslims has led to much fighting between India and Pakistan.

Asia contains one of the world's greatest industrial powers. This is Japan, which is one of the world's most prosperous countries.

In 1991, 77 per cent of Japanese people lived in cities and towns. By contrast, only 27 per cent of the people in India live in cities and towns. Even though India has some of the world's largest cities, including Bombay, Calcutta and Delhi, most Indians are poor farmers who grow little more than they need to feed their families.

The poorest countries in Asia are Bhutan and Nepal, which lie north of India. Bangladesh, Laos and India also rank among the world's 20 poorest countries.

△ *Lamaist monks sit outside their temple in Tibet. Tibetans believe in Lamaism, a kind of Buddhism.*

▷ *A high-speed 'bullet train' passes Mount Fuji near Tokyo, in Japan.*

The Economy

Agriculture employs about 60 per cent of all Asians. The main crops vary according to the climate. The chief food crop in warm, wet regions is rice. The world's top five rice producers – China, India, Indonesia, Bangladesh and Thailand – account for 75 per cent of world production.

In cooler regions, including northern China and Russia, the chief food crop is wheat. Other major farm products include cotton, rubber, sugar and tea.

Asia has many resources. The nations in southwestern Asia, including Saudi Arabia, Iran, Iraq and Kuwait, contain about two-thirds of the world's known oil reserves. Several countries in Asia also have large amounts of coal and many metals.

Japan is one of the world's most advanced industrial countries. Other fast-developing areas include South Korea, Hong Kong, Malaysia, and Singapore. Russia also has many industries, and the number of factories in China and India is growing rapidly. Tourism is also important in many Asian countries.

Hong Kong

Hong Kong has one of the world's busiest ports, and is the tenth biggest trading nation in the world even though it is only 1,070 sq km (413 sq mi) in area. It is renowned for manufacturing textiles, clothing, cameras and electrical goods. Hong Kong, a British colony since 1842, will return to Chinese control in 1997.

◁ *Malaysia produces about a quarter of the world's natural rubber. Rubber is made from latex, a white juice which comes from the rubber tree.*

AFRICA

AFRICA is the second largest continent after Asia. It covers about a fifth of the world's land area. The continent contains 53 independent countries. At the end of World War II in 1945, most of these countries were colonies, ruled by Britain, France, Portugal and Spain.

Africa (53 countries)

Algeria	Central African	Eritrea	Kenya	Nigeria
Angola	Republic	Ethiopia	Lesotho	Rwanda
Benin	Chad	Gabon	Liberia	São Tomé &
Botswana	Comoros	Gambia	Libya	Principe
Burkina Faso	Congo	Ghana	Madagascar	Senegal
Burundi	Djibouti	Guinea	Malawi	Seychelles
Cameroon	Egypt	Guinea-Bissau	Mali	Sierra Leone
Cape Verde	Equatorial Guinea	Ivory Coast	Mauritania	Somali Republic
			Mauritius	South Africa
			Morocco	Sudan
			Mozambique	Swaziland
			Namibia	Tanzania
			Niger	Togo
				Tunisia
				Uganda
				Zaire
				Zambia
				Zimbabwe

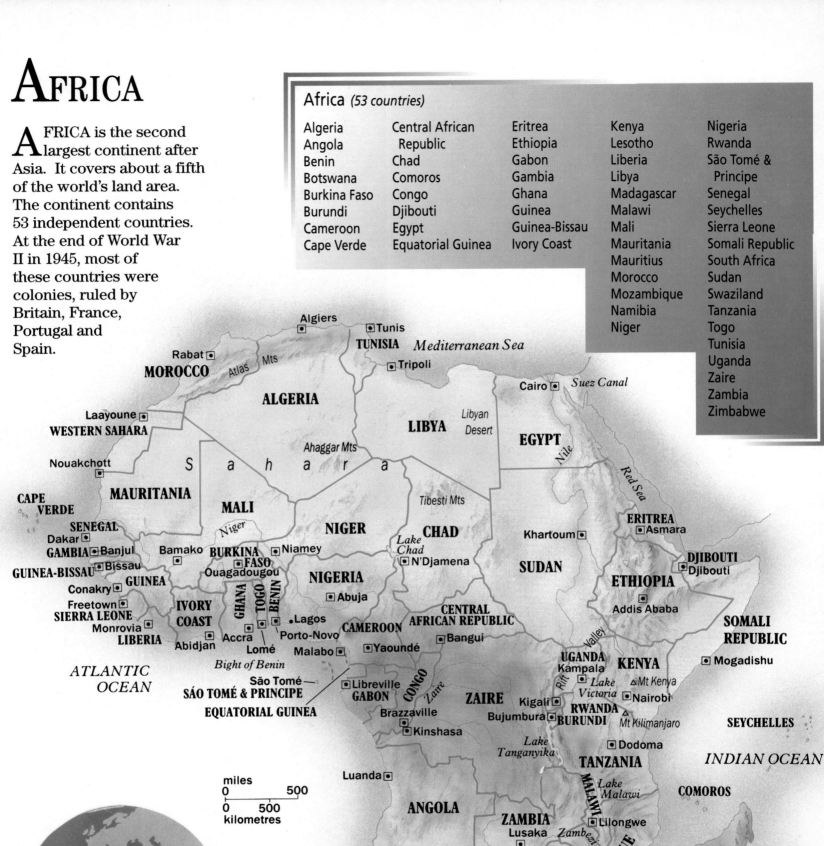

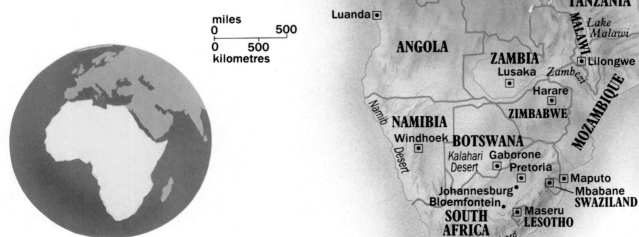

The Land

A huge tableland surrounded by narrow coastal plains makes up most of Africa. In the east, a deep valley cuts through the tableland. It contains long lakes, such as Lake Tanganyika. Great rivers, including the Nile, Zaire and Niger, drain the tableland.

Mountain ranges rise in northwestern and southern Africa, but the highest peaks including Kilimanjaro, are old volcanoes. Africa includes several islands. Madagascar, in the southeast, is the world's fourth largest island.

The Climate

The equator runs through the middle of Africa and most of the continent is hot or warm throughout the year. But the highlands are much cooler than the steamy coastlands.

Africa contains huge deserts, including the Sahara, the world's largest, in the north, and the Namib and Kalahari deserts in the south. Vast rainforests grow near the equator, where the rainfall is heavy. Between the forests and the deserts are grasslands, where elephants,

▷ *The pyramids of Egypt were built around 4,500 years ago. Ancient Egypt was the first great civilization.*

lions and zebras are found.

The climate is mild in the far northwest and southwest of Africa, with hot dry summers and mild, rainy winters.

The People and the Economy

Most of the people in northern Africa are Arabs or Berbers, who speak Arabic and follow Islam. Black Africans live south of the Sahara, where more than 1,000 languages are spoken. Some Black Africans are Christians and others are Muslims, but many follow old African religions.

Africa has some rich resources, such as oil and gas in the north, and gold and diamonds in the south. But most Africans are farmers. Living standards are generally lower than in other continents. Severe droughts sometimes cause starvation.

Africa in brief

Highest point: Kilimanjaro, in Tanzania, 5,895 metres (19,340 feet).
Longest river: Nile, 6,671 kilometres (4,415 miles).
Largest lake: Victoria, 69,484 square kilometres (26,828 square miles).

▽ *Farmers grow food to feed their families. Spare produce is sold in local markets.*

▽ *Warm grasslands lie at the foot of Africa's highest peak, the snow-capped Kilimanjaro in Tanzania.*

AUSTRALIA AND THE PACIFIC

AUSTRALIA is the only country which is also a continent. Australia, with Papua New Guinea, New Zealand and other nearby islands, form a region called Australasia. Australasia, with the many small Pacific islands lying to the east and north, form a region known as Oceania.

The first, or Aboriginal, people of Australia probably came to the continent from Asia more than 50,000 years ago. But most Australians today are descendants of Europeans. Australia has huge cattle and sheep farms. Farm products include fruits, sugar cane and wheat.

Australia in brief

Highest point: Mount Kosciusko, in the southeast, 2,228 metres (7,310 feet).
Longest river: Darling, 2,739 kilometres (1,702 miles).
Largest lake: Lake Eyre, 9,583 square kilometres (3,700 square miles), though it contains water only after heavy rains.

Australia

Australia is a mostly dry and flat continent. The only large mountain ranges are in the east. The east also contains most of the best farmland. Much of western Australia is desert.

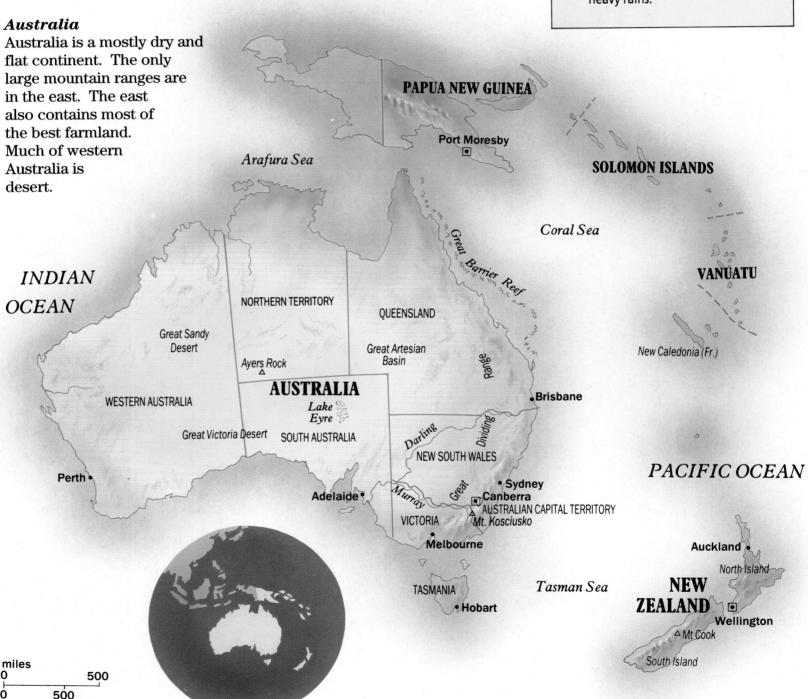

PAPUA NEW GUINEA

Port Moresby

Arafura Sea

SOLOMON ISLANDS

Coral Sea

VANUATU

New Caledonia (Fr.)

INDIAN OCEAN

NORTHERN TERRITORY

QUEENSLAND

Great Sandy Desert

Great Artesian Basin

Ayers Rock

Great Dividing Range

AUSTRALIA

Lake Eyre

WESTERN AUSTRALIA

Brisbane

Great Victoria Desert

SOUTH AUSTRALIA

Darling

NEW SOUTH WALES

Perth

PACIFIC OCEAN

Adelaide

Murray

Great Dividing Range

Sydney

Canberra

AUSTRALIAN CAPITAL TERRITORY

Mt. Kosciusko

VICTORIA

Melbourne

Auckland

North Island

TASMANIA

Tasman Sea

NEW ZEALAND

Wellington

Hobart

Mt Cook

South Island

miles
0   500

0   500
kilometres

30

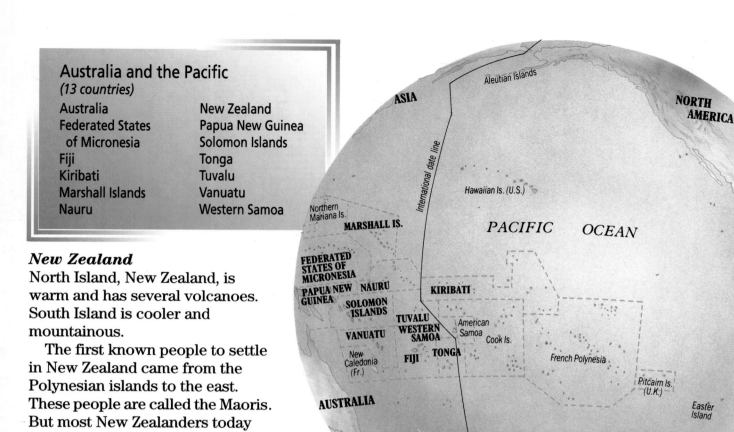

Australia and the Pacific
(13 countries)

Australia	New Zealand
Federated States	Papua New Guinea
of Micronesia	Solomon Islands
Fiji	Tonga
Kiribati	Tuvalu
Marshall Islands	Vanuatu
Nauru	Western Samoa

New Zealand

North Island, New Zealand, is warm and has several volcanoes. South Island is cooler and mountainous.

The first known people to settle in New Zealand came from the Polynesian islands to the east. These people are called the Maoris. But most New Zealanders today are descendants of British settlers. New Zealand is famous for its farm products, including butter, cheese, meat and wool. Forestry is also an important industry.

◁ *Ayers Rock is a famous landmark in the heart of Australia.*

▷ *Melanesians live in Papua New Guinea, north of Australia.*

The Pacific Islands

There are three main groups of Pacific islands: Melanesia, Micronesia and Polynesia. Melanesia means 'black islands'. This refers to the dark skins of the people. Melanesia includes Papua New Guinea, the Solomon Islands, New Caledonia, Fiji and Vanuatu. Micronesia means 'tiny islands'. This region includes the Marshall Islands, the Federated States of Micronesia and Nauru.

Polynesia mean 'many islands'. This group of islands sprawl across a huge area, including Tonga, Western Samoa, Kiribati and French Polynesia. Hawaii, in the north, also belongs to Polynesia, as also does Easter Island, a Chilean territory in the east.

31

THE HUMAN WORLD

HUMAN ACTIVITIES, such as farming and the building of cities, industries and roads, have changed the appearance of many parts of the world.

Farming

Farming is the world's most important industry. It supplies food and other essential items used for clothing and shelter, which everyone needs.

Crop farming is limited to only about

a tenth of the world's land area, while another fifth is used for pastoral, or animal, farming. The rest of the world's land area is unsuitable for farming, being too cold, too dry or too rugged. These areas contain few people.

People first began to grow crops about 11,000 years ago in the Middle East. As food became plentiful, some people gave up farming and moved to settlements where they worked in new craft industries. This change in human society was the first step towards urban civilizations.

Cities

The earliest cities were founded about 5,500 years ago. Today, most people in the richer, developed countries live in cities and towns, but most people in poorer, developing countries still live in rural areas.

For example, 75 per cent of the people in the United States live in urban areas. By contrast, in India, 73 per cent of the people live in rural areas. Many Indians are poor farmers who produce little

more than they need to look after their families.

Cities are centres of industry. Many city people are employed in manufacturing industries. But

△ *Manufacturing micro-chips takes great care. They become the 'brains' of computers and robots, which are replacing people in may jobs.*

◁ *The world's growing population is a heavy burden on the Earth's resources. Children in poorer countries like India (left) are seen as future breadwinners. Governments must improve the lives of the poor and encourage them to have fewer children.*

Human activities map key

	Cereal grains
	Rice
	Mostly uncultivated
🍊	Fruit
🐄	Cattle
🐑	Sheep
	Most populated areas
	Most populated areas in cereal growing regions
	Most populated areas in rice growing regions
★	Cities above 10 million people
▪	Cities above 5 million people

Pastoral Farming

Pastoral land, where farm animals are raised, covers about a fifth of the world's land area. Animals are usually kept on land which is unsuitable for crops. Sheep rearing is important in New Zealand, right, which has about 20 times as many farm animals as people.

schools, than people in rural areas. But they also suffer pollution, noise and traffic jams. Human progress has had a major impact on our world, causing great destruction of nature in many areas.

▽ *The overgrazing of grasslands in central Chad, Africa, has helped turn large areas into desert. Here, herdsmen draw water from a well.*

in many countries, even larger numbers work in service industries, such as government, health, finance or education. In the United States, the world's richest country, farming and manufacturing are highly efficient.

In the early 1990s, farming employed only 3 per cent of the labour force, while industry employed 26 per cent.

Many people in cities are wealthy. They often enjoy better services, including hospitals and

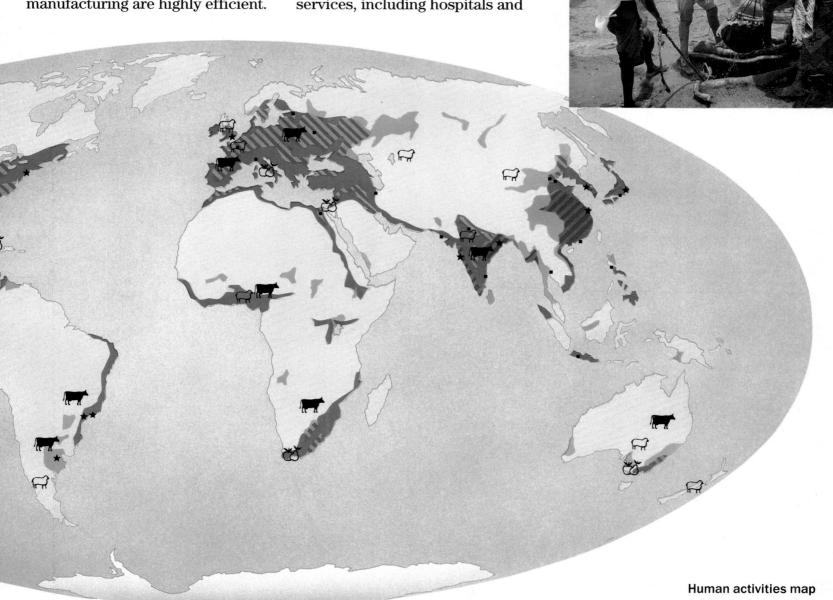

CLIMATE

THE CLIMATE of a place is its usual, or average, weather. A place in a desert may have heavy rainstorms every few years. But if its average rainfall is less than 250 millimetres (10 inches) per year, then that place is described as a desert.

Climatic Factors
Every place has a different climate, depending on where exactly on the Earth it is. Places near the equator are generally warmer than places near the poles. Mountains affect climate, because high land is colder than nearby lowland. Even on the equator, snow always covers the highest mountaintops. The summit of Mount Kilimanjaro, in Tanzania, is covered with snow all year round.

Climate is also affected by the ocean currents. For example, the Gulf Stream, which flows from the Gulf of Mexico, warms the climate of northwest Europe. Places near the sea usually have milder climates than places far inland.

World Climates
Different places around the world can have similar climates. For example, deserts cover huge areas of Africa, Australia and North America. The climate in these areas is hot and dry.

The climate in continental regions is neither very hot nor very cold. In warm continental regions around the Mediterranean Sea, the summers are long and hot and the winters cool and wet. Cold continental climates, found in much of Europe, Russia and North America, have cooler summers and snowy winters.

In the tropical regions, on either side of the equator, the climate is divided into two: rainforest areas, with rain throughout the year, and tropical grasslands, which have a marked dry season.

The coldest parts of the Earth are the regions around the North and South Poles. The climate in these places is very harsh. The temperature is below freezing point for most of the year, and snow and ice cover the ground. Even during the summer, when it is always light at the poles, the sun cannot melt the ice-caps.

△ Northern England has a cool temperate climate.

◁ The Sahara is the world's largest desert. Parts of it are covered by huge hills of sand, called dunes. Desert people travel from place to place to find water for themselves and their animals.

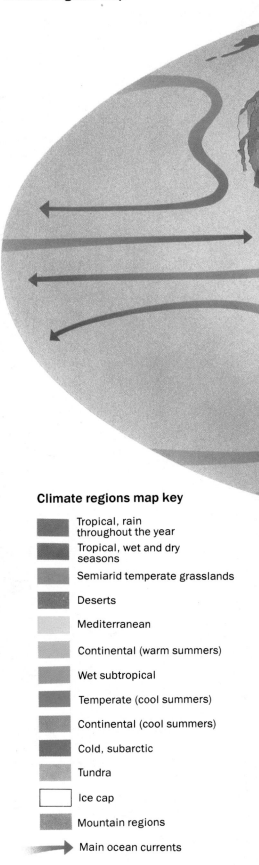

Climate regions map key

- Tropical, rain throughout the year
- Tropical, wet and dry seasons
- Semiarid temperate grasslands
- Deserts
- Mediterranean
- Continental (warm summers)
- Wet subtropical
- Temperate (cool summers)
- Continental (cool summers)
- Cold, subarctic
- Tundra
- Ice cap
- Mountain regions
- → Main ocean currents

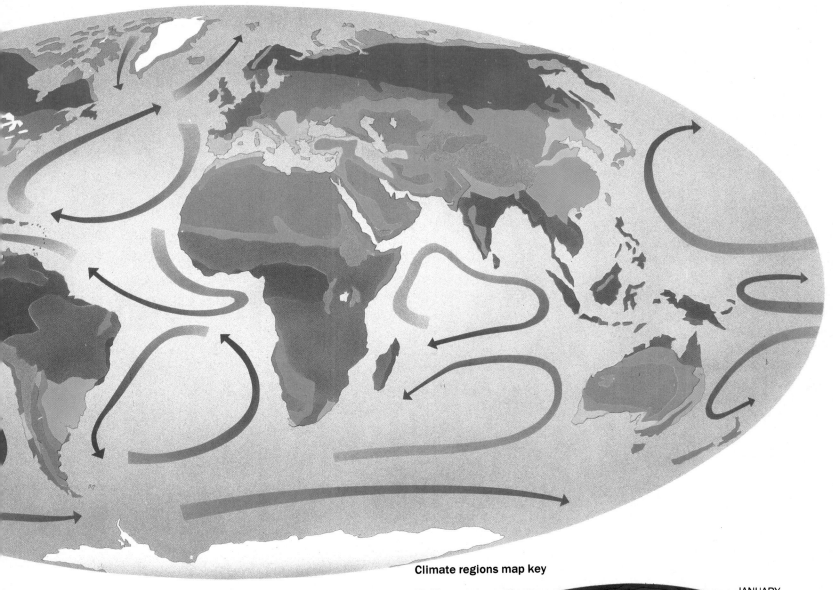

▷ The maps show the average January and July temperatures throughout the world. Temperatures and rainfall are the two main factors that determine the climate of any place.

▽ The map shows the average yearly rainfall in different parts of the world.

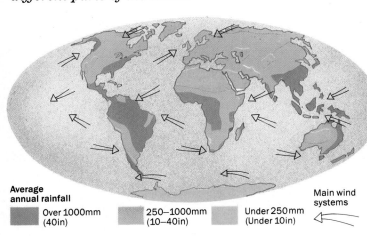

Average annual rainfall

Over 1000mm (40in)

250–1000mm (10–40in)

Under 250mm (Under 10in)

Main wind systems

Climate regions map key

World average temperatures

°C	°F
−45	−49
−35	−31
−25	−13
−15	5
−5	23
0	32
5	41
15	59
25	77
30	86
35	95

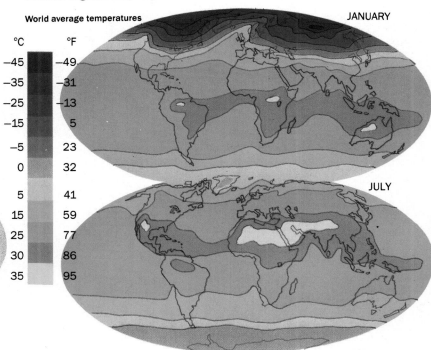

JANUARY

JULY

THE ENVIRONMENT: POLLUTION OF LAND, SEA AND ATMOSPHERE

IN THE LAST 200 YEARS, the damage that people have done to the environment has increased dramatically. This is partly due to the building of large industrial cities and partly because of the growth in the world's population from about 1,200 million in 1850 to more than 5,000 million today.

Land Pollution

Soil is often polluted by pesticides which kill the bacteria and other creatures that make the soil fertile.

The cutting down of forests and the overgrazing or the over-farming of land removes the protective cover of grass and roots on the ground. As a result, the soil is often blown away by the wind or washed away by running water. Sometimes, fertile areas, such as the dry grasslands south of the Sahara, become deserts.

Water Pollution

Some factories dump poisonous wastes in rivers, killing living things and endangering people. Some factory wastes reach the sea and pollute coastal waters. At sea, wrecked oil tankers sometimes spill huge slicks of floating oil, which destroy marine life.

Air Pollution

Factories, power stations and cars produce poisonous gases which cause smog. These gases contain

Land and sea pollution map key

- Existing desert
- Areas at risk from desertification
- Tropical rainforest
- Rainforest seriously damaged in recent years
- The most polluted seas
- The most polluted rivers
- Sites of known nuclear accidents

Rainforest destruction

Rainforests contain more than half the world's plants and animals, and produce much of the oxygen we breathe. Their destruction is a serious threat to our planet.

Air pollution map

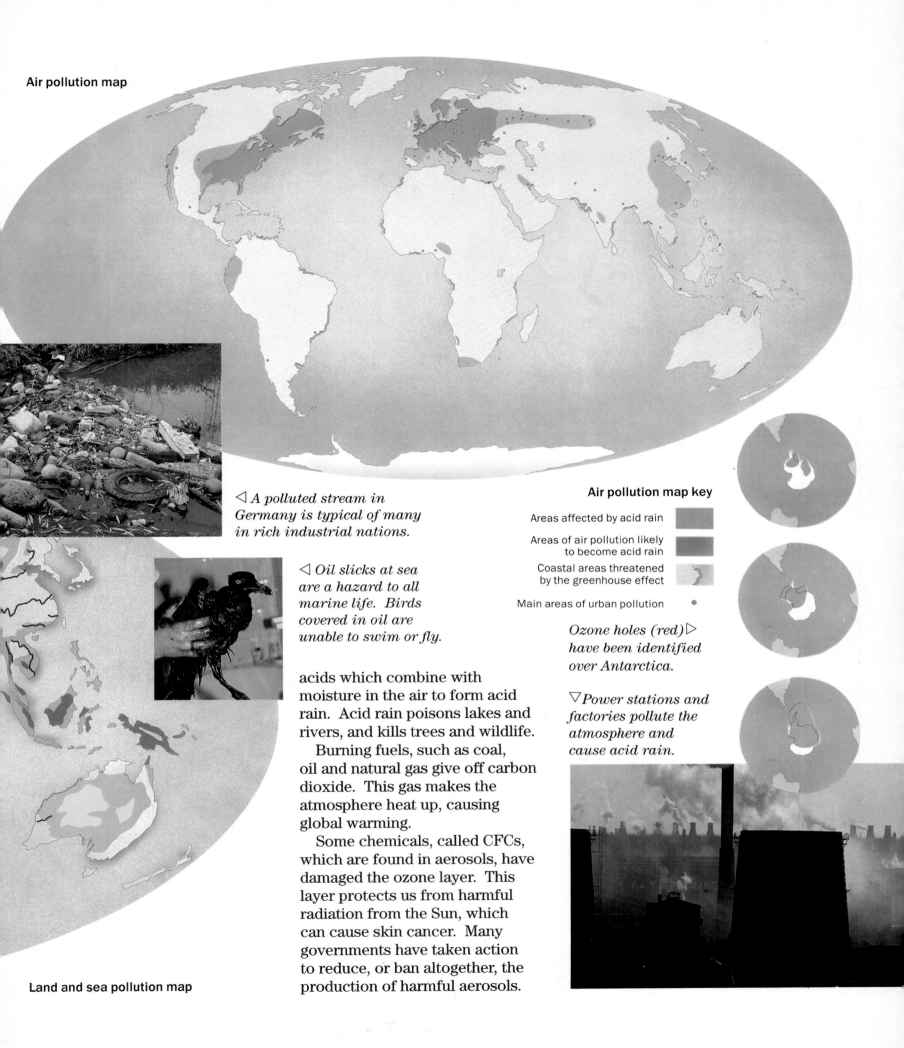

A polluted stream in
Germany is typical of many
in rich industrial nations.

Oil slicks at sea
are a hazard to all
marine life. Birds
covered in oil are
unable to swim or fly.

Air pollution map key

Areas affected by acid rain

Areas of air pollution likely
to become acid rain

Coastal areas threatened
by the greenhouse effect

Main areas of urban pollution

Ozone holes (red)▷
have been identified
over Antarctica.

▽Power stations and
factories pollute the
atmosphere and
cause acid rain.

acids which combine with
moisture in the air to form acid
rain. Acid rain poisons lakes and
rivers, and kills trees and wildlife.
 Burning fuels, such as coal,
oil and natural gas give off carbon
dioxide. This gas makes the
atmosphere heat up, causing
global warming.
 Some chemicals, called CFCs,
which are found in aerosols, have
damaged the ozone layer. This
layer protects us from harmful
radiation from the Sun, which
can cause skin cancer. Many
governments have taken action
to reduce, or ban altogether, the
production of harmful aerosols.

Land and sea pollution map

WORLD INFORMATION TABLE: INDEPENDENT COUNTRIES

p. – page numbers refer to location on main continental maps

p.	Country	Area sq km	Area sq mi	Population	Capital
24	Afghanistan	652,090	251,773	21,558,000	Kabul
17	Albania	28,748	11,100	3,338,000	Tiranë
28	Algeria	2,381,741	919,595	26,375,000	Algiers
17	Andorra	453	175	60,000	Andorra la Vella
28	Angola	1,246,700	481,354	9,732,000	Luanda
15	Antigua & Barbuda	440	170	81,000	St. John's
15	Argentina	2,776,889	1,068,302	33,099,000	Buenos Aires
22	Armenia	29,800	11,506	3,499,000	Yerevan
30	Australia	7,713,364	2,978,147	17,540,000	Canberra
17	Austria	83,853	32,376	7,906,000	Vienna
22	Azerbaijan	86,600	33,436	7,145,000	Baku
15	Bahamas	13,878	5,358	263,000	Nassau
24	Bahrain	678	262	532,000	Manama
25	Bangladesh	143,998	55,598	112,832,000	Dhaka
15	Barbados	430	166	259,000	Bridgetown
22	Belarus	207,600	80,155	10,346,000	Minsk
17	Belgium	30,519	11,783	10,039,000	Brussels
15	Belize	22,965	8,867	200,000	Belmopan
28	Benin	112,622	43,484	5,042,000	Porto-Novo
25	Bhutan	47,000	18,147	1,497,000	Thimphu
15	Bolivia	1,098,581	424,165	7,527,000	La Paz
17	Bosnia & Hercegovina	51,129	19,741	4,383,000	Sarajevo
28	Botswana	581,730	224,607	1,360,000	Garborone
15	Brazil	8,511,965	3,286,488	153,850,000	Brasilia
25	Brunei	5,765	2,226	273,000	Bandar Seri Begawan
17	Bulgaria	110,912	42,823	8,952,000	Sofia
28	Burkina Faso	274,000	105,792	9,537,000	Ouagadougou
28	Burundi	27,834	10,747	5,818,000	Bujumbura
25	Cambodia	181,035	69,898	9,010,000	Phnom Penh
28	Cameroon	475,442	183,569	12,245,000	Yaoundé
8-9	Canada	9,976,139	3,851,809	27,344,000	Ottawa
28	Cape Verde	4,033	1,557	389,000	Praia
28	Central African Republic	622,984	240,535	3,166,000	Bangui
28	Chad	1,284,000	495,755	5,977,000	N'Djamena
15	Chile	756,945	292,258	13,599,000	Santiago
25	China	9,596,961	3,705,408	1,166,144,000	Beijing
15	Colombia	1,138,914	439,737	33,405,000	Bogotá
28	Comoros	2,235	863	510,000	Moroni
28	Congo	342,000	132,047	2,428,000	Brazzaville
15	Costa Rica	51,100	19,730	3,135,000	San José
17	Croatia	56,538	21,829	4,773,000	Zagreb
15	Cuba	110,861	42,804	10,841,000	Havana
24	Cyprus	9,251	3,572	715,000	Nicosia
17,19	Czech Republic	78,841	30,441	10,383,000	Prague
17	Denmark	43,077	16,632	5,166,000	Copenhagen
28	Djibouti	23,200	8,958	465,000	Djibouti
15	Dominica	751	290	72,000	Roseau
15	Dominican Republic	48,734	18,816	7,321,000	Santo Domingo
15	Ecuador	283,561	109,484	11,028,000	Quito
28	Egypt	1,001,449	386,662	54,805,000	Cairo
15	El Salvador	21,041	8,124	5,389,000	San Salvador
28	Equatorial Guinea	28,051	10,831	437,000	Malabo
28	Eritrea	117,600	45,406	3,318,000	Asmara
17	Estonia	45,100	17,413	1,554,000	Tallinn
28	Ethiopia	1,104,300	426,373	50,527,000	Addis Ababa
31	Fiji	18,274	7,056	750,000	Suva
17	Finland	338,145	130,559	5,062,000	Helsinki
17	France	551,500	212,935	57,338,000	Paris
28	Gabon	267,667	103,347	1,201,000	Libreville
28	Gambia	11,295	4,361	929,000	Banjul
22	Georgia	69,700	26,911	5,493,000	Tbilisi
17	Germany	356,910	137,804	80,553,000	Berlin
28	Ghana	238,533	92,098	15,824,000	Accra
17	Greece	131,990	50,962	10,454,000	Athens
15	Grenada	344	133	91,000	St.George's
15	Guatemala	108,889	42,042	9,746,000	Guatemala City
28	Guinea	245,857	94,926	6,048,000	Conakry
28	Guinea-Bissau	36,125	13,948	1,002,000	Bissau
15	Guyana	214,969	83,000	806,000	Georgetown
15	Haiti	27,750	10,714	6,715,000	Port-au-Prince
15	Honduras	112,088	43,277	5,418,000	Tegucigalpa
17	Hungary	93,032	35,920	10,202,000	Budapest
17	Iceland	103,000	39,769	261,000	Reykjavik
25	India	3,287,590	1,269,346	883,476,000	New Delhi
25	Indonesia	1,904,569	735,358	184,274,000	Jakarta
24	Iran	1,648,000	636,296	59,791,000	Tehran
24	Iraq	438,317	169,235	19,184,000	Baghdad
17	Ireland	70,284	27,137	3,536,000	Dublin
24	Israel	21,056	8,130	5,113,000	Jerusalem
17	Italy	301,268	116,320	57,844,000	Rome
28	Ivory Coast	322,463	124,504	12,841,000	Abidjan
15	Jamaica	10,990	4,243	2,394,000	Kingston
25	Japan	377,801	145,870	124,318,000	Tokyo
24	Jordan	97,740	37,738	3,949,000	Amman
22	Kazakhstan	2,717,300	1,049,156	16,954,000	Alma-Ata
28	Kenya	580,367	224,081	25,838,000	Nairobi
31	Kiribati	726	280	75,000	Tarawa
24	Kuwait	17,818	6,880	1,400,000	Kuwait
22	Kyrgyzstan	198,500	76,641	4,472,000	Bishkek
25	Laos	236,800	91,429	4,384,000	Vientiane
17	Latvia	64,500	24,904	2,617,000	Riga
24	Lebanon	10,400	4,015	3,781,000	Beirut
28	Lesotho	30,355	11,720	1,860,000	Maseru
28	Liberia	111,369	43,000	2,719,000	Monrovia
28	Libya	1,759,540	679,362	4,873,000	Tripoli
17	Liechtenstein	160	62	30,000	Vaduz
17	Lithuania	65,200	25,174	3,754,000	Vilnius
17	Luxembourg	2,586	998	389,000	Luxembourg
17	Macedonia	25,713	9,928	2,172,000	Skopje
28	Madagascar	587,041	226,658	12,384,000	Antananarivo
28	Malawi	118,484	45,747	9,085,000	Lilongwe
25	Malaysia	329,749	127,317	18,610,000	Kuala Lumpur
24	Maldives	298	115	228,000	Male
28	Mali	1,240,192	478,841	8,962,000	Bamako
17	Malta	316	122	360,00	Valletta
31	Marshall Islands	181	70	50,000	Majuro
28	Mauritania	1,025,520	395,956	2,082,000	Nouakchott
28	Mauritius	1,865	720	1,099,000	Port Louis
15	Mexico	1,958,201	756,066	84,967,000	Mexico City
31	Micronesia, Federated States of	702	271	108,000	Palikir
22	Moldova	33,700	13,012	4,359,000	Chisinau
17	Monaco	1.9	0.7	30,000	Monaco
25	Mongolia	1,566,500	604,829	2,311,000	Ulan Bator
28	Morocco	446,550	172,414	26,262,000	Rabat
28	Mozambique	801,590	309,496	16,565,000	Maputo
25	Myanmar (Burma)	676,578	261,228	43,718,000	Yangon (Rangoon)
28	Namibia	824,292	318,261	1,529,000	Windhoek
31	Nauru	21	8	9,000	——
25	Nepal	140,797	54,362	19,892,000	Katmandu
17	Netherlands	40,844	15,770	15,167,000	Amsterdam
30	New Zealand	207,986	104,628	3,415,000	Wellington
15	Nicaragua	130,000	50,193	3,916,000	Managua
28	Niger	1,267,000	489,191	8,171,000	Niamey
28	Nigeria	923,768	356,669	101,884,000	Abuja

p.	Country	Area sq km	Area sq mi	Population	Capital
25	North Korea	120,538	46,474	22,614,000	Pyongyang
17	Norway	323,895	125,057	4,281,000	Oslo
24	Oman	212,457	82,030	1,647,000	Muscat
24	Pakistan	796,095	307,374	119,347,000	Islamabad
15	Panama	75,517	29,157	2,514,000	Panama City
30	Papua New Guinea	462,840	178,704	4,055,000	Port Moresby
15	Paraguay	406,752	157,048	4,519,000	Asunción
15	Peru	1,285,216	496,225	22,370,000	Lima
25	Philippines	300,000	115,831	64,189,000	Manila
17	Poland	323,250	124,808	38,365,000	Warsaw
17	Portugal	92,389	35,672	9,843,000	Lisbon
24	Qatar	11,000	4,247	524,000	Doha
17	Romania	237,500	91,699	22,865,000	Bucharest
21-22	Russian Federation	17,075,400	6,592,849	148,920,000	Moscow
28	Rwanda	26,338	10,169	7,310,000	Kigali
15	St.Kitts-Nevis	261	101	42,000	Basseterre
15	St.Lucia	622	240	156,000	Castries
15	St.Vincent & the Grenadines	388	150	104,000	Kingstown
17	San Marino	61	24	24,000	San Marino
28	São Tomé & Principe	964	372	121,000	São Tomé
24	Saudi Arabia	2,149,690	830,000	15,909,000	Riyadh
28	Senegal	196,722	75,955	7,845,000	Dakar
28	Seychelles	455	176	69,000	Victoria
28	Sierra Leone	71,740	27,699	4,354,000	Freetown
25	Singapore	618	239	2,814,000	Singapore
17	Slovakia	49,035	18,933	5,346,000	Bratislava
17	Slovenia	20,251	7,819	2,017,000	Ljubljana
30	Solomon Islands	28,896	11,157	385,000	Honiara
28	Somalia Republic	637,657	246,201	8,302,000	Mogadishu
28	South Africa	1,221,037	471,445	39,763,000	Cape Town; Pretoria; Bloemfontein
25	South Korea	99,016	38,230	43,663,000	Seoul
17	Spain	504,782	194,897	39,077,000	Madrid
24	Sri Lanka	65,610	25,332	17,396,000	Colombo
28	Sudan	2,505,813	976,500	26,587,000	Khartoum
15	Surinam	168,265	63,037	467,000	Paramaribo
28	Swaziland	17,364	6,704	860,000	Mbabane
17	Sweden	449,964	173,732	8,707,000	Stockholm
17	Switzerland	41,293	15,943	6,864,000	Bern
24	Syria	185,180	71,498	12,961,000	Damascus
25	Taiwan	36,000	13,900	20,727,000	Taipei
22	Tajikistan	143,100	55,251	5,634,000	Dushanbe
28	Tanzania	945,087	364,900	25,965,000	Dodoma
25	Thailand	513,115	198,115	57,992,000	Bangkok
28	Togo	56,785	21,925	3,899,000	Lomé
31	Tonga	747	288	101,000	Nukualofa
15	Trinidad & Tobago	5,130	1,981	1,268,000	Port-of-Spain
28	Tunisia	163,610	63,170	8,405,000	Tunis
24	Turkey	779,452	300,948	58,467,000	Ankara
22	Turkmenistan	488,100	188,456	3,852,000	Ashkhabad
31	Tuvalu	26	10	10,000	Fongafale on Funafuti atoll
28	Uganda	235,880	91,074	17,475,000	Kampala
19,22	Ukraine	603,700	233,090	52,118,000	Kiev
24	United Arab Emirates	83,600	32,278	1,668,000	Abu Dhabi
17	United Kingdom	244,100	94,248	57,701,000	London
8,9	United States	9,809,431	3,787,443	255,414,000	Washington, D.C.
15	Uruguay	177,414	68,500	3,131,000	Montevideo
22	Uzbekistan	447,400	172,742	21,285,000	Tashkent
30	Vanatu	12,189	4,706	155,000	Port-Vila
17	Vatican City	0.44	0.17	1,000	—
15	Venezuela	912,050	352,145	20,310,000	Caracas
25	Vietnam	331,689	128,066	69,225,000	Hanoi
31	Western Samoa	2,831	1,093	162,000	Apia
24	Yemen	527,968	203,850	13,128,000	Sana
19	Yugoslavia*	102,173	39,449	10,597,000	Belgrade
28	Zaire	2,344,858	905,355	39,794,000	Kinshasa
28	Zambia	752,618	290,587	8,589,000	Lusaka
28	Zimbabwe	390,759	150,873	10,352,000	Harare

* Consisting of the former Yugoslav republics of Montenegro and Serbia

POPULATED DEPENDENCIES

Australia (A) Chile (C) Denmark (D) France (F) Netherlands (N) New Zealand (N.Z.) Portugal (P) United Kingdom (U.K.) United States of America (U.S.A.)

p.	Dependency	Area sq km	Area sq mi	Population	Capital
31	American Samoa (U.S.A.)	199	77	39,000	Pago Pago
†	Anguilla (U.K.)	96	37	7,000	The Valley
†	Aruba (N)	193	75	61,000	Oranjestad
†	Azores (P)	2,344	905	250,000	Ponta Delgada
†	Bermuda (U.K.)	53	20	52,000	Hamilton
†	Cayman Is. (U.K.)	259	100	24,000	Georgetown
†	Channel Is. (U.K.)	195	75	147,000	St. Helier; St. Peter Port
31	Cook Is. (N.Z.)	236	91	17,000	Avarua
31	Easter Island (C)	122	47	2,000	—
†	Faeroe Is. (D)	1,399	540	48,000	Tórshavn
15	Falkland Is. (U.K.)	12,173	4,700	2,100	Stanley
15	French Guiana (F)	90,000	34,749	96,000	Cayenne
31	French Polynesia (F)	4,000	1,544	207,000	Papeete
26	Gaza Strip	378	146	658,000	Gaza
17	Gibraltar (U.K.)	6	2	32,000	Gibraltar
6	Greenland (D)	2,175,600	840,004	58,000	Godthab
15	Guadeloupe (F)	1,705	658	400,000	Basse-Terre
†	Guam (U.S.A.)	541	209	150,000	Agana
25	Hong Kong (U.K.)	1,045	403	5,805,000	Victoria
25	Macao (P)	16	6	487,000	Macao
†	Madeira Is. (P)	797	308	253,000	Funchal
†	Man, Isle of (U.K.)	588	227	67,000	Douglas
15	Martinique (F)	1,102	425	366,000	Fort-de-France
†	Midway Island (U.S.A.)	5	2	500	—
†	Montserrat (U.K.)	98	38	12,000	Plymouth
†	Netherlands Antilles (N)	800	309	194,000	Willemstad
30	New Caledonia (F)	18,575	7,172	175,000	Nouméa
†	Niue Island (N.Z.)	260	100	2,500	—
†	Norfolk Island (A)	36	14	2,000	—
31	Northern Mariana Is. (U.S.A.)	477	184	47,000	Saipan
†	Palau, or Belau (U.S.A.)	497	192	15,000	Koror
	(Also called Trust Territory of the Pacific Islands)				
31	Pitcairn Is. Group (U.K.)	5	2	60	—
15	Puerto Rico (U.S.A.)	8,897	3,435	3,554,000	San Juan
†	Réunion (F)	2,510	969	611,000	Saint-Denis
†	St. Helena Group (U.K.)	314	121	7,000	Jamestown
†	St. Pierre & Miquelon (F)	242	93	6,000	St. Pierre
†	Tokelau (N.Z.)	12	5	2,000	—
†	Turks & Caicos Is. (U.K.)	430	166	11,000	Grand Turk
†	Virgin Is. (U.K.)	153	59	17,000	Road Town
†	Virgin Is. (U.S.A.)	342	132	97,000	Charlotte Amalie
†	Wake Island (U.S.A.)	8	3	300	—
†	Wallis & Futuna Is. (F)	200	77	14,000	Mata-Uta
26	West Bank *	5,860	2,263	973,000	—
28	Western Sahara **	266,000	103,577	162,000	El Aaiún

† Not shown on map   * Claimed by the Palestine Liberation Front: occupied by Israel

** Claimed by Morocco and Polisario Front: occupied by Morocco

PLUTO   NEPTUNE   SUN   EARTH   MARS

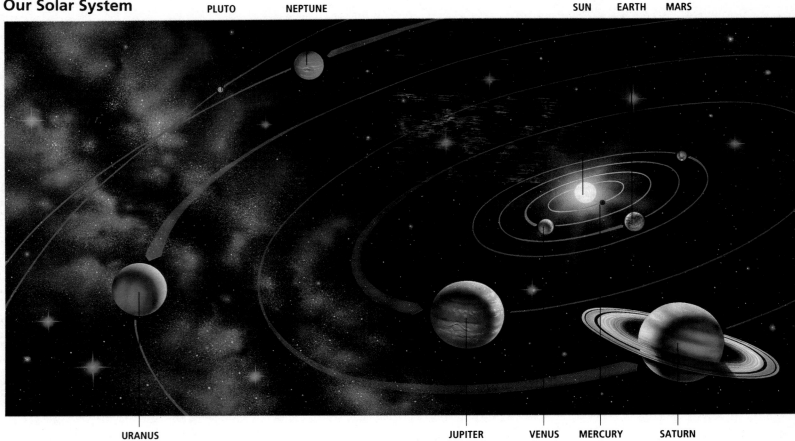

URANUS   JUPITER   VENUS   MERCURY   SATURN

▽ *The world is divided into 24 main time zones. People change their watches by one hour as they cross* *from one zone into another. Time zones are measured east and west of 0° longitude. There is a difference of 24 hours at the International Date* *Line. People crossing this line heading west lose a day. People going east gain a day.*

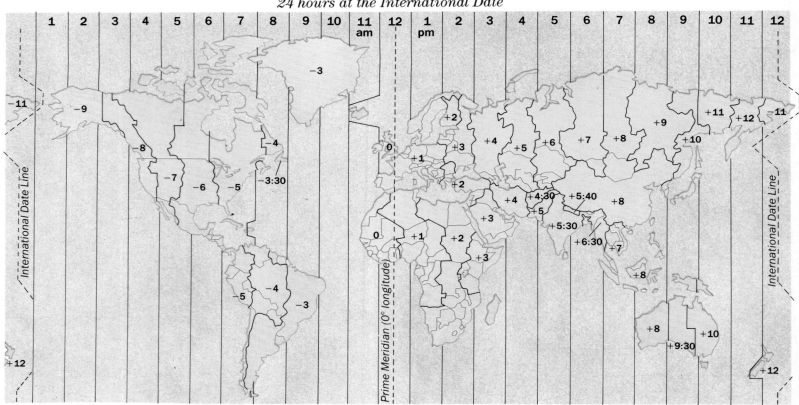

← Lose a day
Gain a day →